They Molested My Mind!

Quanjay J. Jones

ISBN (EBook): 978-1-7331159-1-9
ISBN (Paperback): 978-1-7331159-0-2

They Molested My Mind is a gripping tale of one young man's stolen innocence. Through vivid details and imaging, author Quanjay Jones shares his story and experience. This story begs you to pay attention. Pay attention to your children and your family members. There is a reason they are behaving in the manner that they are. Care enough to ask them if everything is okay and then listen and believe them. This book is a gift – one that deserves to be re-gifted. Make a commitment to help someone take back the power of their life.

Tamika L. Sims
Editorial Review

Dedication

First and foremost, I thank God for his direction in my life

I dedicate this book to everyone who played a role in my life, whether good or bad. Your role helped shape the person I've become. If your role was a negative one, I want you to know that I forgive you with my whole heart and wish you nothing but the best. I would like to thank my mother, who taught me how to make wise decisions; I love you and wish you were still here with me. I want to thank my bishop, Duane Greene for fathering me, showing me how to be a man of God and for helping to shape my destiny. Lastly, I dedicate this book to everyone whose minds have been molested by a life of trials and tribulations. I pray that your healing begins as you read my story and you learn to forgive yourself and your past. May God bless you and forever be with you!

Contents

CHAPTER 1

He Tricked Me!

"Let me get two green leaf Dutch Masters and your cheapest lighter. Oh yeah, and that two eleven right there is mine too!" I reached into my pocket to hand the clerk some money, pulling the rubber band off the stack of bills I had in my hand. I flipped through them until I got to a five, handed it to her, and then told her to keep the change. I grabbed my bag, dapped my homie up that came into the store, walked outside and got into my '89 Champagne Cadillac Deville. The seats were so far back that I had to lean to the side just to see as I drove. I rode with my left hand on the top of the wheel and my elbow resting on the center console, music bumping loud, listening to some beats that I'd made, freestyling about anything I thought of.

With one hand still on the wheel, I reached for the ounce of weed that I had stashed in the glove compartment and started to break up enough buds to fill one of the blunts I picked up from the store. By the time I got home, I was ready to roll up! I got out of the car and walked into the bricked-in, doublewide trailer on a pond that we were renting. I walked into the room, turned on some Bob Marley and listened to him sing 'No Woman No Cry' until I got settled in and ready to twist up!

I grabbed the book that I used to roll weed on and prepared myself for the masterpiece I was about to create. With my two thumbnails, I split the Dutch down the middle and threw the guts in the ashtray. I licked the edges of the blunt for handling purposes, then sprinkled weed down its center. Looking like a professional cigar maker, I tightly rolled the blunt to keep everything in, yet loose enough to smoke evenly without over-burning. I saturated the outside of the blunt with saliva to create a seal during the drying process.

I used a lighter to heat the outside of the blunt just long enough to dry it and activate the seal, preventing it from unraveling as I smoked. The moment of truth had arrived. Flick! Flick! I put the flame to the tip of the blunt as I held the other end with the edge of my lips. I closely observed the Dutch, taking it out of my mouth, putting it back in again, while still holding the lighter's flame to the tip of it.

I cautiously took in the first wave of smoke as I laid my head back on the bed. The aroma filled the room as I puffed a few more times. I started to feel the euphoric feeling that relaxed my mind and body. I smiled as the satisfaction of the high overcame me, but this time was different. This high was not like the rest. Usually I would just sit back and allow my mind to drift off into nothingness, thinking about outer space, aliens and ghosts. I would be jumpy from hearing things outside, thinking that the cops were about to pull up at any moment and bust my operation.

But this time, I thought about why I was getting high in the first place. Such a weird thought process. What caused me to want to get high? I mean besides the normal excuses of why I told myself that I was getting high. My excuses were usually, "To relax my mind," or, "Get rid of some stress." For some reason, I felt the question deserved a different response this time. Usually someone else would ask me why I smoke weed, but this time I asked myself the question. I couldn't pacify myself with the usual answer, the question deserved something more this time. I hit the blunt again and began to think hard about it. Why did I smoke so much anyway?

I took a few more hard hits and I heard a voice say, "You are running from something!" So, I asked myself, "What am I running from?" At this point, I didn't know much about God. I didn't grow up in church. I didn't know Jesus. All I knew about church was vacation bible school and dressing up for Easter. I didn't know anything about God leading, guiding, or instructing you, or that you could even talk to Him like that.

But when I asked myself the question, "What am I running from?" there was no answer. I started to think about things that I could be possibly running from. I started asking myself questions. Why do I get so stressed? What bothers me the most? Why am I always sad? Why don't I have any friends? Why do I prefer to be alone? Why do I seek the approval of others? Why am I not confident in myself? What causes me to hate? Why do I want to kill people? What happened to compassion and where did love go? Why do I always want sex and can't seem to get enough? Why can't I trust?

Who, what, when, where, how, why, can and if were the questions that bombarded my thoughts. My mind raced back and forth, around and around. It was like watching Jeff Gordon on a race track inside my head. I hit the blunt again and yelled out, "Son of a sap sucka!" I had burned my fingers as I pulled and dropped the roach on the book that I used to roll on. After recuperating from the burn, I rolled another blunt. After a couple of pulls from the spliff, I started to see myself as a teen just a few years ago.

Flashes of situations, let-downs, disappointments and hurt feelings sprung forth like a light was just turned on. The visions went further and further back in time, until I could see myself as a little boy and suddenly tears started to roll down my cheeks. I remembered it as if it was yesterday; the first time the real world showed itself, it was the summer of 1988. It was hot in South Carolina that year. The heatwaves seemed to cast shadows as vapors rose from the concrete, disappearing into the air.

******

I grew up in a neighborhood called Burnswood, located in the city of Columbia, SC. It was an urban neighborhood. Most of the people barely got by, but there were a few well-off, middle-class families. Crackheads walked the streets day and night. Drug dealers hung out at the nearest 'dope boy' house or corner store. Women walked around in short shorts and kids played amongst them all. There was gambling, bike racing, car racing, drunken foot races, dog fights, shoot outs, fist fights, knife wounds, death and break-ins. This was the environment that I was born into and spent the most critical years of my life adapting to.

That summer seemed to be one of the hottest on record. It was over 100 degrees and the humidity was high. The only kids outside were the ones who didn't have air conditioning in their homes and that's because the house was usually hotter than it was outside, even with the windows up. I was in luck to be good friends with a guy by the name of Dean, who was my next-door neighbor. Dean was five years older than me, but neither of us cared and our parents didn't either. He was the only child of his mother for a while, so he got all the good stuff – games, toys, basketball goal, good snacks, name-brand clothes and shoes.

I kind of looked up to Dean because he was good at everything. He always seemed to beat me no matter how hard I tried. Even when I took my shoes off he still won at racing and beat most of the other kids too. He was great at basketball and always talked about going to University of North Carolina to play in college. Needless to say, I learned how to play ball by getting my butt beat so much.

I was always around Dean. He was like a big brother and when we had fights that sent me home crying, we would usually be outside playing again before the end of the day. Sometimes I really miss those days; the days when you can get mad at your best friend, have an all-out brawl and be best friends again the next day. Back then a sorry wasn't even needed, it was just understood when one of us came to the other's house and asked, "You want to come outside?"

At five years old I was plump and round, but always outside roaming the yard looking for my next adventure. I made mud pies, dug holes, chased cats and climbed trees. You might not believe it, but I even tried to fly one day! I tied a pillow case around my neck, thinking that Superman's cape is what gave him power, and I figured that if I tied it tight enough, it would really work. So, with the pillow case snug, I climbed to the highest step on my porch, ran as fast as I could, and jumped! I didn't fly, and I learned a valuable lesson that day; the higher you climb, the louder the thump when you hit the ground!

I did a lot of interesting and questionable things as a child, but it was all innocent fun. I got away with a lot because I was the baby boy and often got what I wanted. But that year we had a special visitor from the hospital – it was a boy! I don't really remember my mother being pregnant at all. It seems like I was the baby boy one day and then I wasn't the next. Even though I had two sisters and an older brother, when my little brother arrived, no one really seemed to notice me anymore. People always said, "He's so cute," and "He has pretty eyes," and "Look at those pink lips." Blah! Blah! Blah! I tried to be helpful around the house to get more attention. I cleaned, took the trash out, helped Mom cook and swept the floor.

One thing I noticed about adults was their need for the mail. I would always hear my mom ask my sisters or brother, "Did you check the mail?" I had a bright idea one day! Thinking that checking the mail would get me kudos or a "thank you son!" I anticipated my mother's arrival and wanted to have the mail ready for her when she got home; before she could ask for it. Parents were always making a big deal about the arrival of the mail, making it seem like it was so important. In my mind, getting the mail would make me important as well. That was the goal anyway. I plotted, planned and waited for the day that I could go get the mail.

One day I was sitting on the porch and saw the mailman coming down the street. I thought I would seize the opportunity to get the mail and become important again. It seemed like there were a thousand mailboxes before he got to my house, but it was only about six houses from the top of the hill to my house, which was at the bottom of the hill. The mailman pulled up and I hid behind a bush so that he couldn't see me. He opened the lid to the mailbox, he reached his hand in and the mission commenced!

As I walked down the driveway, I couldn't help but feel a sense of freedom. Five years old, doing something on my own, without being told and without supervision. Usually my mother would watch me from the screen door after she told me to check the mail or she'd stand in the driveway to make sure I was safe, but on this day a man was being born. The mailbox was mine and if anybody was going to get that mail today, it was going to be me! I wanted to do it without being asked or told to get it. This was my rite of passage. This was the day that I made my own decisions. This was the day that would mark the beginning of who I would become forever.

The mailbox was just a few steps away when my neighbor, David M. Lester, began to wave his hand. I threw my hand in the air and proceeded to the mailbox. I stood in front of the mailbox and just stared at it, as if I was waiting for it to say, "Enter my son!" My hand reached up to open the lid and I felt like I was about to open a treasure chest full of gold at the end of a rainbow. This was it! The moment when a boy becomes a man and leaves behind his need to be watched or supervised. My hand went inside the box like a snake closing in on its prey! After a few pats inside the box and standing on my tippy toes to look inside, I found nothing. I wondered why the mailman stopped if he didn't put anything in there. I saw his hand go in, so what happened to the mail?

Suddenly, a feeling of hopelessness came over me as I looked up at the steep driveway before me. Walking back with nothing in my hand was going to make the climb even harder. Before walking up the driveway, I saw David standing at the edge of his yard, looking at me. When I noticed him, he started to walk over towards me. It was like he took one step, then suddenly he was right behind me. He was a fifteen-year-old, dorky-looking kid, with feminine tendencies and he talked with a lisp. He must have been watching me play or something, waiting for the opportunity to ask me the famous question that most of them ask, "Do you want some candy?"

To a fat, five-year-old kid, or any other kid for that matter, asking them if they want candy is like fishing with a freaking net! The fish don't even get a chance to play with the hook and take a little piece of worm off, tasting the sweetness of its meat before deciding to take the whole bait! Net fishermen trap fish as they are swimming by, not suspecting a thing. Then suddenly, swoosh! The fish are ensnared and tossed into a boat, out of their natural environment, placed in a holding tank until they are killed, eaten or sold to the highest bidder.

To ask a child if they want candy is like swinging a net over their heads while screaming, *Gotcha*! What kid doesn't love candy? Of course, I said yes! I had known him all my life and he had given me candy before, so there was no reason for me to be alarmed.

After I said yes, he took my hand and led me to his house across the street. We walked across his stumpy, patchy yard with leaves covering it from the previous fall season and I tripped a little as he pulled me forward towards his house. After walking up the steps of the front porch, holding on to the raggedy wooden rails for support, he opened the door to his home and ushered me in.

His mother, sister and father were sitting in the den area watching television. The room was dark. They had blankets covering the windows to prevent the sun from shining through. The only light available came from the occasional bright light of the TV as the screen changed from one scene to the next. His family was so busy yelping and laughing at the TV that they didn't notice as he walked behind me going up the stairs to his room. We walked right past them and they didn't even see him take me upstairs. I don't think they even noticed him coming into the house, but I always believed that his sister saw me go up there with him and didn't say anything.

Once we got into the room, he told me that the candy was under the bunk bed and that he couldn't reach it. Since I was small enough to reach it, he suggested that I should go under there and get it, then we could split it. I didn't ask any questions about the candy, like why didn't he just pull out the bed and get it? My mouth was already salivating from the thought of Tootsie Rolls, Laffy Taffys and Cow

Tales, and the little caramel rounds with the white cream in the middle that everyone in the neighborhood usually went to the corner store to get. All I could think about was how I was about to have a good ole time with my candy.

I remember wanting to ask why he didn't pull the bed out. However, that could have just been a question I thought about as the years went by. A question that, if I had asked myself that day, maybe the events that happened next would not have occurred.

I got on my knees to look under the bed and I told him that I couldn't see anything. He told me that it was in the back, towards the wall and that I had to go under there to get it, so that's what I did. After inching my way partially under the bed with just my feet sticking out, David pushed me all the way under the bed and came in behind me. I didn't have much time to react or think. After he had gotten under the bed, he pulled out his penis and started stroking himself. He then told me that he wanted me to put it in my mouth. I told him that I didn't want to, but he grabbed my head and pulled me towards this thing that looked like a baby snake sticking out of a patch of grass.

David started trying to align my head with this bush of hair. He pushed my face closer and closer, telling me to suck it like a sucker and he would give me the candy. He placed his penis on my lips and told me, in a firm voice, to stick out my tongue, so I stuck out my tongue. I wasn't too fond of its taste, so I told him that it was nasty, then he said something that haunted my thoughts for years. He said, "If you do me, I will do it to you next." I really don't know why he thought a five-year-old child would enjoy a blow job, but I guess in his sick and twisted world, I would.

I really didn't want his penis in my mouth and, even though I didn't know what was going on, it was clear to me that I wanted it to stop immediately. He didn't consider the stain that he was going to leave on my life after he had satisfied his lustful desires. He didn't think about what he was teaching me, or that I might grow up wanting to slice his throat like a chef filleting a steak. He just wanted to leave the stain of his loins on the inside of my stomach and around my mouth.

After telling him I wanted to stop, he put his hands on the back of my head and without saying a word he pushed it back down on his penis. He sounded and looked as though he enjoyed what he made me do. His eyes began to close, and his head fell back. At that moment a sudden thought came over me like a jolt of electricity passing through my body. I wondered how it would feel for him to do it to me. This thought changed my life. Even though I was only five years old, at that moment I wanted someone to put their mouth on me. Maybe I would enjoy it like he did. Maybe I would utter groans of pleasure at the cost of my dignity and moral code. So, I asked him, "Is it my turn now?"

I wonder how many people who have been molested had that same thought; the feeling of wanting to do to someone what is being done to you? Maybe therefore the molested become molesters; in some vain attempt to understand why someone enjoyed taking their innocence and forcing them to do sexual acts against their will. Maybe the molested are attempting to get back what was stolen from them. Future events would prove that this thought might be more dangerous than safe, more disturbing than settling, and more life altering than changing.

What David made me do must have only lasted for five minutes, but it seemed like a lifetime under that bed. I wanted it to stop. I wondered what this was in my face, in my mouth, and why he enjoyed it. I had never even looked at my own penis at that time. I did not know what it was capable of. But at that moment, I knew that what I had down there can make me feel great! Before David could get the result that he wanted to see on my face, his brother Ron came into the house calling for him. Ron burst into the house like a bat out of hell and came running up the stairs screaming his name, "David! David! David! Where are you?"

Ron walked in the room and started calling for David franticly, almost like he knew I was in there with him, under that dark bed, closed off from the world, trapped in front of a body four times bigger than my own, unable to move or make a sound. David had put his hand over my mouth and put his finger up, signifying my silence, concealing his little game.

"David!" his brother screamed, standing at the top of the stairs. He called down to his mother, asking if she had seen him, and of course she said no. Then Ron ran down the stairs and David hurried me from under the bed, pulling me out like he was playing tug of war. He stood up and pulled me to my feet, grabbing my shoulders and hoisting me up like a rag doll.

David told me not to tell anyone what he had done to me or he would kill me. He pulled at the slightly closed door that was left open after his brother ran out frantically searching for him. I walked down what seemed to be the longest staircase in the world. I looked back and saw David walking behind me, brushing himself off, pulling his shirt down, trying to conceal his erection.

Before I got to the bottom of the stairs, I turned around and asked him for the candy he promised, but he nudged me in the middle of my back, between my shoulders, with his knee, pushing me on down the stairs. Of course, there was no candy and I felt betrayed more than anything else. As I neared the bottom of the steps, I saw Ron standing there talking to his mom and dad. As I got ready to go out the door I was stopped by David's mom, and Ron said, "I just came up there looking for you."

David said, "We were hiding."

"Hiding from what?" Ron replied, and a moment of silence struck the room.

Ron's mother asked me what we were doing, and I looked at David, who looked back at me, and I said, "Nothing." We all looked at each other, anticipating more questions, but David tried to make up some lame excuse. Then Ron's parents told him to walk me back home safely. Ron asked if I was okay and watched me walk across the street. Leaving their house, I could hear the faint sounds of arguing and yelling. I didn't know what they were saying, but it had to have been about me being upstairs alone with him and what he did to me.

Maybe Ron was being molested as well and he saw that monster take me away like a thief in the night. Maybe he knew what was about to happen and came to my rescue before anything else bad could happen. Maybe he got a quickening in his spirit that something was wrong and came to investigate the feeling that plagued him. I've always wondered what made him come into the room, calling for his brother at the time he did. Who knows what would have happened to me next, or what David would have made me do?

I walked across the street towards my house, kicking rocks along the way, upset that I didn't get the candy I was promised and feeling robbed because David didn't get to do me like he said he would. I thought I was in trouble and I had nothing to show for it. I was lied to and I felt used. I quickly learned that I didn't like being lied to or used. As for that dreadful act that David made me do, I didn't think anything else about it. I didn't really know that it was wrong for him to do that to me and I thought I would get in trouble if I told anyone. I never said anything about what happened to me that day and I went back to being a kid, or I thought I did.

CHAPTER 2

See What He Started!

After my innocence was stolen from me, sex was now a sought-after event in my life. I wanted to experience its pleasures and have someone do to me what David made me to do him. I had never gotten my turn and I wanted that turn now more than ever. I wanted to feel what he felt. I wanted to do what he did and moan pleasures that I didn't even know existed. My eyes were now open to a whole new world; one that I was blind to before that tragic and terrible day. This world bound me in shackles and seemed to hold me hostage. I saw sex everywhere after the day I was tricked.

It was hidden like secret passages in a castle within the social conversations of grownups while they played Spades and Tonk for money on Friday and Saturday nights. It was everywhere I looked and there was nothing I could do about it. To tell you the truth, I didn't want to do anything about it. I wanted to learn more. What was it that they were talking about so much?

One day while I was jumping up and down on my big brother's bed, I jumped too high and came down so hard that the mattress slid forward. My legs flew in the air as I fell back and hit my head. I got up dazed but noticed a stack of magazines underneath the mattress as I tried to straighten the bed up before my brother got home. I pulled one of the magazines out and saw a naked girl. I had hit the jackpot!

It was the holy grail of things a young boy could find. I felt like I had found gold at the end of the rainbow. Finally, I could see what the fuss was about or at least see what the big secret was. I looked around outside the room to see if anyone was coming and tiptoed back to the bed. I lifted the mattress and opened the magazine. My eyes started to grow big and wide as I flipped through the pages. I saw women doing what that guy made me do to him, and then I started to understand why he made me do it. I kept flipping pages and every time I thought I heard a noise I would drop the mattress down and sit on the bed as fast as I could, pretending to look innocent.

Ignoring the magazines or pulling one out and going to a secret place would have been easier to do rather than trying to hold the mattress up with my head and use two hands to flip through the pages, but I didn't think of that. I was too intrigued by what I had found. I was like a moth to a flame. I was attracted helplessly to something that had the potential to burn me and leave me scarred. Now I was curious about what was under every mattress. I was hip to the secrets that lie beneath the bed, the things that people hide, the places people keep secrets. I looked under my older sister's mattress and found more sex magazines and quickly realized that sex was a normal part of life. I looked under my mother and stepfather's mattress and found all kinds of goodies, including more sex magazines.

My mind became filled with all kinds of images, positions and nasty words that grownups used. Days and weeks went by and I learned all about sex. I now knew fully and completely what I possessed between my legs and knew also that it was a weapon to be used for my own pleasure. But why was mine so much smaller than the guys' in the magazine? Will it get bigger? I was now six years old and learning about sex. I was young, tender and impressionable. I soaked it all up like a sponge the size of Texas.

I can remember watching the rap duo Salt-n-Peppa on TV and getting aroused by their movements on the video of their latest hit. Sex was quickly becoming the highlight of my life. It became an everyday event, something I looked forward to seeing. I looked for it in my surroundings. I will never forget the day I saw my sister's friend with a broomstick between her legs and the guy acting like it was his penis while they grinded back and forth on the stick. I thought that girl was so sexy, and I wanted her for myself. I wanted her to grind with me the way she did with that guy. But she just thought I was cute; not knowing the thoughts I was conjuring up inside my little head.

Now that I had seen grinding for the first time, which seemed to be equally as pleasurable as sex, I wanted to try it. I got myself a little girlfriend from my first-grade class who was very pretty. We rode the bus together, sat beside each other every day and we kissed on the lips like adults. Even though they were little pecks here and there, we thought we were doing big things. I would feel on her like I saw other teens and adults doing, then I started to introduce her to my world.

One day I convinced her to get under the seat with me and I got on top of her and started to grind like I had seen my sister's friends do. We thought we were having sex and it felt good! That went on for months until I pulled out my 'thang'. She ended up telling her mother, who told her she couldn't have a boyfriend at that age, and she stopped being my friend altogether. Then a few weeks after that she moved away, and I didn't see her again.

I was sad for a little while, but I wasn't giving up hope just yet. My sister's best friend at the time had a niece named Hope, who became my girlfriend. I was only seven years old, but since I couldn't get an older girl who would do the things I saw, I had to get one my age and teach her how to do the things I needed her to do. After my first little girlfriend had moved, I quickly got another one. I was hip to the game. I had to be sneaky and fast like the adults were. I had to move like a stealth plane and do things behind closed doors where no one could see. I needed to hide my guilty pleasures like they hid things under their mattresses.

By the time I was seven years old, I had already come into contact with sex, drugs, guns, murder, mayhem, alcohol, cigarettes and gangs. I'd seen people running and hiding from the police, women abused in front of my eyes, and everyone seemed to accept it as the norm. My mind was quickly becoming corrupt from all the practices that were being accepted as a way of life. It was all a part of my culture and no one told me it was wrong to do these things, mainly because they were doing them too. In fact, everyone looked as if they were having fun.

Women got the brakes beat off them and still stayed with the guy. I did what everyone else showed me was okay.

I can remember times when Hope and I would be playing together and touching each other at the same time. We had a crawl space under the steps of the garage at my house. Hope and I went under there one day and we tried to have sex. She pulled down her pants, I pulled out my 'thang' and I tried to put it where I had seen the guys sticking it in the magazine.

We didn't know what we were doing, and I will never forget her telling me to "get it up" and I replied, "I can't get it up!" We kept trying until we got tired of grinding, and when I did get some blood flow, I couldn't put it inside of her because it wouldn't go in. I didn't know lubrication was required at the time to enter a woman. I just tried to do the things I saw others doing.

I felt the warmth of her flesh next to mine as I tried to put my penis inside her and it felt good. Unfortunately, our past experiences taught us that sex was good and we didn't think about our ages at the time. We just wanted to enjoy what we saw grownups smiling and talking about. We had many sexual encounters over the next year or two and each time our touching escalated. The first time I showed that I cared about her was when we were walking to the bus stop together and she was shivering. I took off my sweater, placed it around her shoulders and held her close.

That same day in school she came to me, gave me my sweater back and said that she was breaking up with me for another guy because his penis was bigger than mine. The bad-boy fifth-grader was really supposed to be in the seventh grade, so of course it would be bigger.

I became angry after that. I was hurt that my second-grade girlfriend left me the way she did, over a bigger penis. I had developed an attachment to her that I thought was love, but when that bond was broken, and she did it with no remorse or regret, it caused something in me to break. I started to hate her, and I was angry. Nothing mattered to me anymore. I was an excellent student before then, being at the top of all my classes, but I started to lose interest.

I was the first to learn cursive writing in second grade, I finished my work faster than the other kids and I was very competitive. I wanted to be the smartest and the brightest. I and this girl named Jessica would see who could finish our work the fastest as we copied sentences from the board, and when we were done, we'd sit there and watch the others as they continued to write.

Jessica and I competed for the best grades from kindergarten to third grade. After being heartbroken at such an early age, I no longer desired to go outside and play anymore, because the girl that broke my little heart lived two doors down, and I didn't want to see her. When I did see her, my anger towards her led me to pick on her. I hit her and caused other kids in the neighborhood to not want to play with her, and then she moved away. I was sad when she moved and felt like I was to blame. Later I learned that she moved for other reasons. But the hurt from that event caused me to look at women differently, even at a tender age.

To get over my ex-girlfriend and show her a thing or two, I got another girlfriend. She was the girl that I had everything in common with, Jessica. We had been together two weeks when a classmate named Trey got jealous that she chose me over him and started to pick on me. He incited other friends to pick on me and one day they jumped me. When I went to fight back, I learned that the guy my first girlfriend left me for was the leader of their gang. He came to Trey's defense every time I got ready to defend myself. His name was Trevon, and he was much bigger and older than the other kids. Everyone was afraid of him because he never lost a fight. As he and the others picked on me severely for years, others started to notice, and it became cool to pick on me. They called me fat, too black, and tried to grab my fatty breasts. School became hell for me and I dreaded going there every single day.

After a couple months of becoming a punching bag and being picked on, Jessica no longer wanted to be my girlfriend. She became Trey's girl, and because of that I hated him. I hated him for a long time. After Jessica stopped talking to me in the second grade, it seemed like the whole school was tormenting me. Even the nerdy kids who usually got picked on, picked on me. I moved in the shadows of life, hoping to dodge the darts that were being shot at my heart every day. But that didn't work.

When school let out for the summer I was happy for a different reason than most kids. I was glad that the picking, nagging and constant abuse had stopped. After the summer of second grade was over, I dreaded going back to school for the third-grade year and it really showed in my work. On the first day of school the torment started, and it happened every day, all day.

I was in constant defense mode; in the classroom, the bathroom, the halls, the lunchroom, at recess, on the bus and even walking home. Kids made fun of my clothes because my family didn't have much money and my haircuts were done with a bowl that my mom put around my head before she cut it, and that made me look uglier than the girls already said I was.

I was bullied by everyone. Even the girls who were bigger than me bullied me, and when I tried to fight back, some of the guys would gang up on me. I did the only thing I knew how to do when someone else was picking on me – I found someone else to pick on. There was a boy who would pick on me when I rode the bus, and the other kids laughed as usual, and I would usually just sit there and take it; but not this time. When we got off the bus I beat his butt.

The kid that I beat up had a brother who was the neighborhood bad boy; well, he was one of them anyway. He was at least five years older than me and even kids his age feared him because of his fighting reputation. He heard about the whipping I put on his brother and came to meet me that morning at the bus stop, but I had already gotten on the bus before he could get there. When he saw the bus pulling off, he shouted some obscenities at me, and I yelled, "Yo Mama!" Why did I do that? He put his fist over his eye and pointed at me as the bus drove away and a fear gripped me that lasted all day. Everybody on the bus knew what that meant. I was going to get it when I got home that day.

School seemed to go by so fast that day. I'd wished that my mom would come and pick me up, but I knew that wasn't going to happen. I tried to play sick so that she could come, but that didn't work. All day kids pointed and laughed at me, telling me that I was going to get my butt kicked after school. I was scared. I was scared because this butt cutting might be worse than the others. My big fat mouth had written a check that my butt couldn't cash, as my mom would say.

The school bell sounded, and I slowly made my way to the bus to face my destiny. The ride was stressful. I thought of every possible way I could escape the beating. Nothing that I came up with seemed as though it would work. Right when I was amid my thoughts with a possible plan that would give me an escape, the bus stopped at my stop. The kids started to get off the bus. I thought about saying I was sorry. I thought about staying on the bus. But as I neared the door to walk down the steps, I put my plan into action.

I stepped off the last step, and as soon as my left foot hit the pavement, I saw him. His eyes locked on me and mine on him, and with my right foot now coming off the step of the bus, I took off like a rabbit running from a hawk. I ran towards a path that went beside my house and I was hauling ass too. I ran so hard that everything around me looked like a blur. My book bag was swinging back and forth, bouncing up and down and I could have sworn that my feet were kicking me in the butt as I ran as hard as I could.

I ran the distance of about fifty yards and had about twenty more to go before I was home, but he had caught up with me and jumped on me. Both of us fell to the ground, he turned me over to face him and I socked him in the jaw! It hurt him too! But when I did that he said, "I wasn't going to hit you, but now I am." He punched me in my head and my stomach then got up and walked away.

The bus driver saw everything and blew the horn for me to come back on the bus. He wanted to drive me home so that no one else could bother me. I don't know why I got on the bus when my house was just a few yards away, but I did. He drove me home and my oldest brother was standing in the street. When I got off the bus crying, my brother John asked me what was wrong. When I told him, he did nothing. He didn't come to my defense, he didn't go beat the boy up, he just asked, "You alright boy?" and sent me into the house.

After that, I knew that I had to learn how to defend myself and I was going to learn on my own. I was tired of the tormenting and jokes. I was tired of getting beat up in school and not doing anything about it. I'd had enough of the running, getting jumped and being pushed off swings. I was ready to do something about it and I did.

While sitting in class one day, Trey started his usual rant about me being fat and having tits. As usual I tried to ignore it, but then I got really upset. I don't know what happened. I guess Trey had said one too many things in class that day because I cursed him something serious and pushed him. After I pushed him, we squared up in the front of the class, waiting on each other to make a move, then someone yelled, "Get him Quanjay!"

I was surprised that someone was on my side. They chanted my name. Who was that? Do I have a friend in this hellhole that I have had to come to for years? When I turned to look in the direction of the chant, I saw a movement out the corner of my eye, much like the spider sense of my favorite hero. As I turned back around to face my challenger I took a punch right on the nose. There seemed to be an eternity of darkness. I saw bright colors of greens, purples, blues and reds, which seemed to last for minutes, but it was only one or two seconds of being dazed.

When I opened my eyes, they filled with tears. I was enraged and attacked everything in front of me. The substitute teacher had already grabbed Trey so that I couldn't get to him and I was furious that I didn't get a chance to show the class what I was really made of. The only thing they saw was a fat boy with tits get punched in the face and it made my last year at elementary school even worse. They didn't care that I was sucker-punched; all they saw was me get rocked. I learned my lesson that day, and that never happened again, ever!

Because of those incidents with girlfriends, I wouldn't have another girlfriend until my junior year in high school. I didn't think that I could trust women. I thought that they were cold, heartless beings, that didn't care about what men felt, only what they themselves wanted. I had many girls interested in me, but I could never allow myself to be vulnerable again. I would pick on girls, make them mad and treat them like the scum of the earth if they liked me. Not because that was how I really felt about them, but because it was easier than telling them I feared being hurt again.

One can't imagine the sensitivity of a boy at a young age and how the sentiment of pain at an early age, if that hurt is misunderstood and misguided, can cause a boy to flee from love for the rest of his life. A young man's broken heart is enough to change his future. It can alter the road that he chooses to walk. Choices are often designed by the culture in which we live. Our environments are like blueprints to our future and all it takes is the wrong or right decision to alter the image of that model.

No one knows what goes through the mind of a child and why they think the way they do. But I am sure that it was something that they witnessed or experienced that caused them to be the way they are, even as adults. I know why I became a person that could kill; it was because of Trey. After the day he punched me on my nose, my eyes were opened. That blackout woke me up! I wasn't the same after that. I wanted to kill him. His name stuck with me. I remembered his face. His eyes glowed in the back of my mind like night lights in the dark.

I spent years taking my anger out on other guys that posed a threat to me; guys that reminded me of Trey. I hated light-skinned men because Trey was light-skinned, and I told everyone else not to trust them. I figured every light-skinned man was sneaky, a backstabber and unworthy of my friendship. It wasn't until I began to remember those events that I realized why I didn't like certain types of guy, based on the characteristics of other men who hurt me. I was doing the same thing that a lot of people do and I was picking my friends that way.

******

I rolled another blunt and thought about the revelation I'd had. I started to understand the *why* behind who I was; I started to understand myself a little more. Then I remembered the hurt of another guy who took something from me.

CHAPTER 3

He Took It!

During my youthful sexual experiences there was someone that I looked up to. His name was John and he was my hero. He was in the ROTC (Reserve Officer Training Corps) and always looked like a soldier in his uniform. I will never forget seeing him in a parade, dressed like a soldier ready for battle. He was swinging that rifle around like it was an extension of his arm, with a serious war look on his face as they marched down the street, between the buildings.

John was a leader in almost everything he did, and I wanted to be just like him. I would get my mother's old broom, unscrew the head off it, leaving just the handle, and go into the backyard to mimic John with his rifle. I would stand in the same spot that he practiced in and twirl my broom handle like it was my own personal rifle. I got good enough to toss it up a few times, until I missed a catch and the broom clocked me on the head.

John was also a magician. Some might say he was into witchcraft or devil worship because of some of the illusions, but I didn't believe that. I remember seeing him do things that most people would not believe were possible or real. I saw him drink gas and nothing happened to him. To prove that it was gas, he poured it in the lawn mower, then cranked it up. John would do all kinds of tricks with cards that baffled the minds of most. He had this one trick where he made cigarette ashes appear out of one hand and into another, which would always freak people out.

One time he drank used motor oil and pulled a white dove out of his mouth; talk about freaky! People would fear or respect him because of the things he did, and I wanted to be like him. I wanted to be both feared and respected. I wanted to know how he did it. How did he pull off those tricks and illusions, or was it real?

I snooped around his room and found a book labeled witchcraft. It had a circle on the front of it, with something that looked like triangles in the middle of the circle. Of course, I didn't really know what that was at the time, so I started reading it. I learned about star rituals, spells and potions. It was cool because it was the same stuff that Mickey Mouse and other Disney cartoon characters did, so it really didn't look that foreign to me.

People say John was weird, but I thought he was gifted. He liked to make things disappear. I remember a story about him that my cousin told me. My cousin said they were playing hide and seek, and he chased John into a bathroom upstairs, but when they opened the door he was gone. We lived in a tri-level house and the bathroom was on the top floor, so there was no way he could have jumped out of the window so quickly at that height. My cousin finished the tale by saying that when they turned to walk out the bathroom, he was behind them as if he had never run into the bathroom in the first place. The whole thing freaked my cousin out and, till this day, they still tell that story.

John loved to make things disappear. I will never forget the first time he made something of mine disappear. It was my Christmas gift and I was six years old. That year my father had bought me a karaoke machine with a tape of my favorite artist, M.C. Hammer. I played that tape over and over and over. I rapped his infamous song as if it was my own and danced as if I was in the spotlight. The spin move I had was sick and no one could touch this. I used to put on a pair of church socks and dance in the kitchen with the mic in my hand like a pop star. I slid all over the floor, spinning and doing that leg shuffle Hammer did; you couldn't tell me nothing.

One day I came home looking for my karaoke machine, ready to get my dance on like I usually did when I got home, but it was gone. I ran up the stairs looking for it because John liked to use it sometimes to listen to his Prince tapes, but it wasn't there! I ran down the stairs into the lower part of our tri-level home calling for Momma, hoping she had seen it.

Mom came running out of the room, "What's wrong with you boy?"

I asked her, "Have you seen my karaoke machine?"

She said, "No, I haven't. Did you check upstairs?"

I said, "Yes, but it wasn't there."

The look on her face let me know that she knew more than she let on, but she said, "I'll find it then."

When John came home, Mom asked him about my karaoke machine and he admitted to pawning it, but the way he said it was as if it was okay for him to do so. Finding out that John pawned my karaoke machine crushed me. It hurt me to my heart and I wanted to kill him. I had heard people saying that John was a thief, but I didn't believe them. In fact, I defended him and got mad when people continued talking about him. That day, my faith in him was ripped away like an old shirt in a street fight. John never apologized, and I never saw that karaoke machine again. I don't know what hurt more, him not apologizing or me never seeing it again and not getting another one.

Unfortunately, John continued to take my stuff without my permission, and other people's things too for that matter. He always did it while I was away, either at school or when I went to my father's house for the weekend. The year after the incident with the karaoke machine, John pawned the TV my father got me for Christmas. It seemed as though I couldn't keep anything of value if John was around, and that made me angry.

Because of John, my father stopped buying me electronic gifts that could be easily pawned, and I no longer received good birthday gifts either. John took my Christmas gifts, my birthday gifts, my sister's things, my stepfather's things and eventually my younger brother's things. John was a selfish person who only cared about himself and what he wanted at that moment. Because of that, I no longer desired to be like him. I lost all faith in the person I thought he was.

When John finally got a good job making a lot of money, he started buying things for the family. I thought for sure that I would get something nice considering all the things he took from me and the hurt he caused, but that was just a figment of my imagination. John bought something for my mother, my stepfather and both of my sisters. My younger brother got a nice name-brand pair of shoes out of the deal, but I didn't get anything. John promised that he would get me something when he got his next paycheck, but he didn't. As the weeks passed, I asked about my gift, but he responded with empty promises and lies.

Eventually I gave up hope. Then I learned that he lost the job because he got caught stealing from them too. I knew that he would never pay me back for the things that he had stolen from me and that I would never be able to keep anything of value if I was too young to defend what was mine.

I didn't trust John much after all the lies and empty promises and I was always suspicious of his actions from then on. I always thought he was up to something and I wanted to catch him in the act. One day I followed him into this valley up the street from my house. Well, I didn't exactly follow him, someone told me that he went there when I inquired about where he was. I had just seen him a few minutes before and now he was gone. I should have known something was wrong when the guy I asked about John gave me the look. You know the look that someone gives you when they are trying to warn you about some place that you aren't supposed to go or should not want to go.

The guy had his head slightly tilted down and to the right, one eyebrow raised like he was imitating the famed wrestler The Rock. His voice had dropped an octave in pitch as to imply a sense of fear associated with the valley, and his chin had doubled as he gazed down at me with big bright eyes saying, "He went into the valley!" I guess he thought I knew what went on in the valley, but I had no clue. So off I went to look for John.

As I neared the front of the valley, I noticed that it was bare, I mean really bare! Grass grew wildly up to the point of the entrance, then stopped. I picked up a stick, thinking that I might have to fight off some wild dogs or something, then I started to walk through the entrance, calling for John.

As I neared the center opening of the valley, I noticed that there was no vegetation anywhere, just big lines that covered the ground and large rocks. It was like walking in the desert or something! The ground was like clay. It was hard, and it seemed to be hotter in that area than anywhere else I had been in the neighborhood.

I kept walking and calling for John. Then suddenly, I started to get the feeling that someone or something was following me. I turned around rapidly, but nothing was there. I started to walk faster, but it seemed like I wasn't getting anywhere. At this point I was no longer concerned with finding John; the only thing I wanted to do was get the heck out of there. I kept feeling like something was right over my shoulder, so I started to get nervous. My heart started beating fast as I felt it creeping closer and closer, but every time I turned around nothing was there.

A tumbleweed blew in front of me like a scene from those old western movies that my stepfather loved to watch. Something was always about to go down when you saw a tumbleweed roll by. I looked towards the entrance where I had come in and the exit where I had never been. The exit was closer than the entrance, so I plotted my course.

As the tumbleweed continued to roll by, a howling sound accompanied it and that struck a fear in me that I would remember for the rest of my life. When I heard the howl, something turned on like a light, and a voice came to me that said, "Run fool!" So, I took off like a bat out of hell! With tunnel vision, I ran for that exit like Speedy Gonzales and I swear it felt like something chased me all the way to the other side where grass was growing again.

As soon as I got to the vegetation, the feeling of being chased and the sense of harm left me. I later found out about a neighborhood rumor, which believed that a cult worshipped the devil in that valley and that it was supposed to be protected by evil spirits!

Ironically, there is an interesting story about that valley being protected. In the entrance of the valley there was a pink panther – a stuffed pink panther, like the big ones you find at the fair. People would always say that if you drove past the valley at night it would be gone. True enough indeed, it was really gone if you drove past the valley at night, but during the day it would suddenly appear again. People in the neighborhood said that the panther walked around guarding the valley during the hours of devil worship. Being that most of us in the neighborhood lived only five minutes away from the place, quite a few people were scared.

One night, my neighbor's dog was barking a very long time, then suddenly popped his chain and began chasing something. This dog was a big German Shepherd, but wouldn't usually get off the chain, though he got off for some reason this night. I and many others were awakened by the most ferocious sounding dog fight I had ever heard. The dog fight must have lasted for about five minutes, or so it seemed, and there was a growl that no one could explain, because it didn't sound anything like a dog. There was barking, then growling from something, then more growling from a normal dog, then the squealing noise a dog makes when it gets hurt, then silence!

The next morning, I went outside to an angry next-door neighbor after hearing a bunch of commotion. My best friend at the time had been crying and his whole family was upset. Their German Shepherd, which was over one hundred pounds, had been mauled beyond recognition. The dog was lying in the garage on its last legs. It looked like the dog had gotten into a fight with something from another planet. I had never seen a dog take a beating like that and I had seen plenty of dog fights. Chunks of skin were ripped from its flesh, fur was missing, legs were broken from being bitten, and blood was everywhere.

There was one question lingering in the atmosphere: Who or what could have done such a thing? Many people always said it was the panther! In fact, after that night, the panther seemed to have disappeared, even during the day, which it had never done before. For years that stuffed animal had sat in that valley during the day, but after that night it was gone. Several days later the big pink panther was back again, but this time it had a tear on its body and we always wondered how it got there, but no one went to investigate it.

Once I had seen what John may have been associated with, I didn't hang around him much after that. I was kind of scared of him myself. He continued taking my things over the years until I was old enough to either fight back, or wise enough to hide my stuff. Darn shame that I had to do so though, but it was either that or risk anything being taken at his free will.

I hated John for taking my things and I wanted to take something from him that he cherished, so I went back to look under the sacred bed. When I looked under his bed, expecting to find the usual sex magazines full of women, I found men having sex with men instead and I was confused for a second. I picked up the book because I thought that I was seeing things, but when I saw the white guy doing to the black guy what David made me do to him, I got angry. I didn't know what being gay really was, but I did know that John was like the guy that had made me do something to him that I didn't want to do, and I no longer cared for John at all.

I didn't know what to think anymore. Everything that I had thought was now a lie. I could no longer believe what he said. Trust was out the door with him and people like him. I started to dislike gay men and I stopped defending him to my friends when they picked on him for being gay. I just didn't care anymore. I just wanted him out of our lives.

CHAPTER 4

She Took My Pride

My mom was the type of person that would give you her last, and sometimes people took advantage of her because of that, but she remained humble and always forgave. People called her 'Nicey', I'm not sure why, but I suspect it was because of her kindness.

My mother was a dark-skinned woman, with full lips. She was big boned at the time, or 'thick' as some would call it, and she was a very intelligent lady. It was like she knew everything. My siblings and I could never hide anything from her or lie to her about anything because she was going to find out one way or the other.

Mom did the best she could raising five children, not really having reliable transportation or a man who was consistently accountable in the home to help take care of things. My stepfather lived with us; however, he was an alcoholic who spent most of his time on the corner at a bar getting drunk. My mom would always have to meet him at his job before he got off to deter him from spending all his money on liquor, which only ended up with them arguing and sometimes fighting.

I grew up in the government housing system. My mom received assistance to help with providing for us, but most of the time the assistance wasn't enough. We received food stamps, but we still ran out of groceries before the end of the month came and had to figure something out so that we could have a meal. Mom would receive her stamps on the first of every month, and if they were late you better believe the social services office knew about it. The first of the month was like food Christmas for us. It was like getting everything a person ever wanted every month.

Naturally, we depended on stamps like cars depend on gas. If they were late for some reason, my mom would call and curse them folk out like they stole something from her, because we usually didn't have food in the house and we didn't have any extra money to buy groceries. My biological father lived only fifteen minutes away from me, but he didn't care whether I was eating or not. He had the nerve to give my mom $25 a month for child support and claimed he didn't have that most of the time. We struggled with hunger a lot when I was younger. We often had to borrow food from neighbors to get by and they also borrowed from us when they didn't have it.

One morning my mom was preparing breakfast, but we didn't have anything to go with the breakfast sausage she was about to cook. She ransacked the kitchen trying to find some grits to go with the only meat we had in the house, but couldn't find anything that would make a meal, so she had to make a hard decision. The look in her eyes was like a runner who had fallen five feet away from the finish line at the Olympics, after being in first place. It was as if someone had cut a chunk out of my mother's side, put it in a casket, dug a grave, buried it six feet deep, covered it with cement, built a fence around it and put a keep out sign in front of it.

She hung her head as she grabbed an old 44-ounce soft drink cup that had Route 44 on the side of it, saying, "Son, I need you to go up the street and ask Mrs. Robinson if I can borrow some grits."

As if my mother didn't feel bad enough, my intelligent self said, "But Mom, I don't want to go. That's embarrassing."

I am sure that was a kick in the shin, along with the punch-in-the-gut decision she had to make. I thought she would get mad at me for saying that, but she said, "I know son, but I need you to go do this for me."

I am sure it would have been more embarrassing for her to take that walk up the street than it was for me, so I said, "Okay." I hung my head as I walked towards the door, dragging my feet every step of the way. Mrs. Robinson lived two houses down, but when I got to the door and looked up the street, her house seemed to be miles away.

My mother followed me as I pushed the screeching screen door open. I proceeded to walk down the stairs on a journey that I would never forget. I looked back to see my mother standing in the doorway, looking at me as if she was sending her son off to war and would never see me again. I crossed the driveway and walked down the narrow dirt path, shaded by a large evergreen tree, towards the street. When I got to the road it seemed like I had only taken two steps and had thousands more to go.

I looked to my right, not to watch for a car, but to see if anyone was looking out of the window of the house across the street. I looked to my left because I was now passing the house of my friend Dean and I petitioned God to provide camouflage for me as I walked up the street with a cup in my hand. As I walked, I flashed back to a time when my next-door neighbor came to my house with a cup in his hand because he wanted to borrow some sugar. I wanted to ask him, "Why don't y'all ever have sugar?" Every time I turned around they needed to borrow some blasted sugar. I promise they made more Kool-Aid than the law allowed, but now the shoe was on the other foot and I was the one needing to borrow something.

Naturally, I thought that someone was looking out the window thinking the same thing about me as I walked up the street with my cup. I gazed intently at the houses in front of me, searching the windows and doors of my neighbors' homes to see if anybody was spying on me. I started to walk faster, feeling as if someone was going to walk outside at any moment.

When I made it without anyone seeing me I was relieved, but now I had another monkey to deal with; I had to ask for the food. I walked up the oil-stained driveway, knocked on the door of Mrs. Robinson's house and waited for her to open the door. After a few knocks, she opened the door, saw the cup in my hand and immediately turned her lips to the side of her face, as if she was saying "Umm hmm" in her mind!

"Come in," she said. I spoke to her as I entered, and she asked, "What you want boy?" But in my mind, I heard her say, "Negro I ain't got it!"

I said, "My momma wanted to know if you had any grits she can borrow." As if we were really going to pay her back in grits. I could sense that she wanted to say no, but I was too cute of a chubby kid and I am sure that I already looked embarrassed enough with my head hung low.

Mrs. Robinson asked, "Did she give you something to put it in?"

I thought to myself, I know you see this darn cup in my hand, but I answered, "Yes ma'am," and handed her the cup. Mrs. Robinson went to her cabinet while giving me instructions to take back to my mom about how to cook grits.

She said, "Tell her I don't have much, so she gone have to put extra water in the pot!"

I said, "Yes ma'am," and received the cup back from her half-filled.

Mrs. Robinson ushered me out of the door. I said thank you and goodbye as I walked down the driveway. Half the battle was won, and the sweet taste of victory was on my lips. Just when I was almost home a neighbor came outside, waved their hand and ruined my victory lap. Darn! Someone had seen me. I was caught! I started to run so fast that I spilled some of the grits on the ground. I turned twenty-two ounces of grits into sixteen in just a few strides.

When I got to my house, my mom thanked me for going, but when she looked at the cup she said, "That's all she gave you? I guess I will have to make do." Of course, I didn't tell her that I had spilled some on the ground while running from the eyes of our neighbors. After all the trouble I went through to get those grits, I was not about to get in trouble for spilling them. I thoroughly enjoyed the breakfast my mom prepared, along with some of her famous biscuits and a can of bulk breakfast sausage that she mixed in with the grits. I dangled my feet and hummed the *Looney Toons* theme song as I ate breakfast and licked the plate after I was done.

After I had gone through that experience, it caused me to be very proud. I didn't want to take anything from anyone. I started becoming self-sufficient and self-sustaining. It had gotten so bad that I didn't even want to take anything from family members. Everyone became victims of my mindset. Sometimes I even offended people and made them upset when they tried to help me out and I declined it, and of course it followed me throughout my life.

I can remember going to my aunt's house to spend time with my cousins and my mom didn't have any money to send with us. I had heard my aunt talking to her husband about not having enough money to pay some bills and do some things in the house and I started to feel way responsible. I started to feel like I was a burden and I wanted to be as far out of the way as possible. I tried to be inconspicuous. I didn't talk much, stayed outside and tried to be the best little boy I could possibly be.

My aunt had to go somewhere. I am not sure where it was, but she loaded us up in the van; her four children, my sister, my brother and me. We went to a few stores, and my cousins, brother and I had a great time in the van, joking and laughing with one another until we pulled into a McDonald's. My aunt ordered all of us a $.69 cheeseburger and everyone wanted one except for me. I thought about the conversation I heard between my uncle and aunt and Mrs. Robinson's facial expression. After remembering the embarrassment of the grits, I vowed not to eat the cheeseburger my aunt bought, despite my hunger. Everyone in the car was eating a burger except me. My stomach was barking, but my pride howled louder as it told me to suck it up.

My aunt tried to make me eat the burger and I declined. I started to cry and continued to voice my discontentment at the idea of that burger entering my mouth, until she turned around with that mommy face. With a stern voice, hair shaking, and head moving, she said, "Quanny, now you gone eat this burger and shut up that fuss." I was mad. I ate the burger, but I didn't like it. I had a frown on my face, but at least I wasn't hungry anymore and the rest of my day was sad as I dealt with the idea of having my pride trampled over again. They took my pride, but I vowed to have victory one day and get to the point where I'd never feel that way again.

CHAPTER 5

She Said, "Sulick It!"

By the time I was eight years old, I had forgotten about what David did to me and really started to like girls. My sister Kathy, who was the youngest of my sisters but older than me, had a friend who was high yellow and thick. She had big breasts, a small waist and a very nice booty. Her name was Katie and she was the neighborhood beauty that all the guys wanted.

She liked wearing denim shorts, and shirts that showed her sexy waistline. She had long hair, which had a brownish tint when the sun hit it the right way, brown eyes and a pretty smile. They said she was a freak. All the guys in the neighborhood talked about wanting to hit that thang. She called me her little boyfriend because I had the biggest crush on her. Even though she was like five years older than me, I thought she was my girlfriend.

I followed my sister around just to be in Katie's presence and got mad when other guys would feel her up, even though she liked to be felt. One day when Katie came over to look for my sister, who wasn't home, she sat there and talked to me for a little bit while waiting for my sister to come back from wherever she was. I believe she had gone to the corner store, but the longer she stayed away, the more personal time I got with Katie.

Katie sat on the porch and made small talk with me. Then, out of the blue, she said, "Hug on me and give me a kiss on the cheek." That was probably one of the best days of my life at that point. After I kissed her on the cheek, she showed me how to kiss a girl on the lips. It was just a soft peck without any tongue, but her lips were as soft as rose petals.

I must have turned her on because what she did next made me a man for sure. This was what every boy dreamed of. It was better than a silly little book with naked women. This was the real deal baby! And they were right in front of me! Two round, soft, salacious breasts were staring me right in the face! She grabbed my hands and allowed me to feel them and I thought I was on top of the world! Those monuments of tissue and fat clothed in silken skin; they felt like love! I mean, if this is what love feels like, then I like love! I want to be in love all the time, I thought.

She popped one of those bad boys out, grabbed my head and told me to suck it! I guess I must have sucked it too hard the first time, because she jumped back a little bit and told me to be gentle. Katie said I had to do it like we kissed. So, I did! Katie grabbed the back of my head and pulled me closer. I couldn't breathe, but I refused to say anything and be forced to stop.

I sucked her breast for a long time. It was enough to make her smile and make me feel like I had done something special. I didn't think she was wrong for giving me something that I needed as a growing boy.

Mom always said, "Milk makes you strong!" In my mind, she gave me something I wanted, instead of something I didn't, like David did.

As I was sucking on Katie's breasts, she grabbed my hand, put it between her legs and coached me on how to rub her vagina. I remember feeling how thick, clean and smooth it was. I felt its warmth and wetness between my fingers, and I liked it. She put a finger inside of herself, then she entered my finger. It made me nervous at first, because I wasn't expecting to feel what seemed like slime. But because it pleased her, it pleased me. After a few minutes, she stopped abruptly, jumped up and went home. I was standing there wanting more of what we were doing, but that was the end of it.

Katie and I never had another sexual encounter after that, but I did catch her looking at my morning wood when my mother sent her upstairs to wake me up for school one morning. I refused to get up after Mom had called my name because I didn't want to go to school. She yelled at the top of her lungs and I laid there like I didn't hear her, squeezing my eyelids closed in case she came upstairs to check on me.

After my mom had called me a few times, she sent Katie, who had been waiting on my sister, so they could walk to the bus stop together. Katie came up the stairs calling my name, "Quanjay!" She had called a few times with no response, so she snatched the covers off the bed, which my younger brother and I shared. I played like I had my eyes closed, squinting just enough to see what she was doing. I saw her looking at my erection like she had never seen one before. Maybe she was surprised that I was so young and had an erection. Maybe she wanted to do something with it, and a part of me wished that she did.

With my eyes squinted, I watched Katie for about thirty seconds before she turned her head at the call of my mom asking her what was taking so long. When she looked back, my eyes were wide open. She bolted out of the room as if she had been caught doing something she shouldn't have been doing and I got up to avoid a butt cutting from my mother before school.

Not too long after that, my sister and Katie had a fight over a nappy head little boy. Katie and I didn't have much communication anymore, not that we had a lot before. I could only see her from the porch as she walked up the street in those sexy clothes she wore and throw my hand up while I gazed at her assets. I guess Katie banished my whole family because of one person. She went on to become the neighborhood freak and I maintained my little crush at a distance.

******

The next encounter I had was with a young woman around the same age as Katie. She was six years older than me. I was at the house and she was in her room moaning. I heard her as I walked by and she called me into the room. Meka was her name. She called me frantically, so I ran fast to get to her, thinking that something was wrong. When I got to her she was lying in the bed with the covers over her. She told me to climb in the bed and I did. Then I asked, "What?!"

She flung the covers off her and I noticed that her hand was on her naked, hairy vagina. She was playing with it like Katie had. Though I didn't know what she was doing, I watched, because I knew it was something that I wasn't supposed to see but wanted to see. She asked me to lick it. I was confused as to what I was supposed to do, but because of everyone making me do things to them sexually, I didn't even question it, I just asked how to do it and did what she told me to do!

I remember it having an odor; a fishy smell, but I thought it was normal. She told me where to lick and how to lick it and I did it. I didn't like it at first, but I guess it grew on me, because she liked it. After a few minutes of doing that and finally getting it right, she asked me to put it in. Mind you, I was only a little boy, but I tried to get it in anyway. I couldn't get it up, so she got frustrated. For some reason, I wanted to please her very badly and I didn't like when I couldn't perform. In the middle of all of that, my friend Dean had knocked on the door and called for me. "Hey Quanjay! You want to come out?"

I guess Dean would have been a better suitor for her because she pushed me off her like she was throwing a rag doll and ran downstairs. I waited there because I thought she would come back, but as I waited I heard multiple footsteps run towards the bathroom and, just as I rounded the corner, I saw her, and Dean enter the bathroom and lock the door.

I had forgotten that he was my friend and I was thrown into a jealous rage. I cried, screamed and beat on the bathroom door for them to come out. I wanted to finish what I started; what I was just introduced to. I felt used and tossed away again, like David did to me and so many others had done. I felt like I didn't get my turn and I wanted it.

I banged on the door for them to come out and Meka poked her head out of the door, telling me to stop beating on the door, but I continued and started to cry and bang on the door after she closed it. Then the door opened again, and I thought, finally! But it was Dean telling me to chill out. They'd be out in a minute and we could play the Sega, but I didn't care about the game.

After my beating on the door for a few more minutes, they came out angry. I was pushed aside as they walked past me like I wasn't even there. Both my friends Dean and Meka left me standing there crying tears of jealousy. I was jealous because each one of them made me do something to them in secret but kicked me to the curb around others. These were feelings and tears that I shouldn't have had at that age. Dean was making me do things to him too. I felt betrayed, but that was a feeling that I would know all too well in my life as the years would pass.

CHAPTER 6

He Took My Friend Away!

The guy who I called my best friend, the one who taught me how to play basketball, football, baseball and so many other sports was now becoming familiar in a way that I didn't like. We used to sit outside and dream about our futures, being rich and having money. We talked about the type of cars we would own, how fast they would go and what color they would be. I loved motorcycles because a dope dealer across the street had one and he would get on that sucker and tear up the road with it, spinning wheels, popping wheelies and even jumping hills. I swear he was either crazy or just too cool. Somewhere along the road, things changed.

Dean and I had the kind of relationship that friends were supposed to have. My little brother would often tag along when he got old enough to hang out, but I had to hold his hand and I didn't like it very much. He interfered with my friendships because my mom would always make me take him along, and he became distracting. He cried all the time and Dean would ask me to take him home every time. My mother would always say, "If your brother can't go, then you can't go." I was forced to play with him instead of Dean. I missed out on a lot of stuff because I had to watch my little brother and I didn't appreciate that at all. It made my life as a kid aggravating.

Dean and I started spending less time together and he started hanging out with teens his own age and talking to girls. I became the third wheel whenever I was around. Dean would only call me over when he didn't have anyone else to talk to or be around; any other time I was kicked to the curb when other people came around. One day our relationship took a drastic turn when he asked me to grab his penis as he started feeling on me.

I was about eight years old at this time and he was thirteen years old when he started touching me. I didn't understand it, but I let it happen because when I didn't want to do what he wanted, Dean got mad and told me to go home. He said if I wanted to play with him and all his things, then I had to do what he wanted.

After he convinced me to let him feel on me, we would hang out. I really didn't understand what I was doing, and I didn't know it was wrong. I just wanted to hang out with my friend. Besides, I had already been made to do things against my will and I saw my older brother with men, so it seemed okay at the time.

As the weeks went by, the touching escalated. Dean started grinding on me in the bushes beside his house, looking around to make sure no one could see us. One day he almost got caught in the yard and he suggested that we go into the house and continue, but I didn't want to. Dean told me to go home and I got sad. I really didn't want to go home because he told me that I could be first on the Sega, so I said that I would go into the house with him.

He asked me to lie down on the floor and I asked why. Dean said, "Just do it. I want to show you something." I laid down and he laid down beside me. He told me to roll over on my stomach and he put his hand under me.

Dean grabbed my penis and told me to move back and forth, so I did. I wasn't sure what I was supposed to get out of doing this with him, but he kept asking me if it felt good and I would reply, "No!" After he removed his hand, he asked for my hand to do the same thing. He obviously enjoyed it because he closed his eyes and started to bite his lip.

After about two or three minutes I said, "Can we go play the game now?"

Dean replied, "Not yet," and he continued to hunch my hand. Because of my previous molestations and the experiments with sex on my own, I was beginning to think that this was normal. I thought that maybe this was what I was supposed to do. Maybe this is what people do when they care about you. Maybe this is what friends are supposed to do together when they are hanging out. I asked about playing the game again and he raised his voice and said, "Not yet," as if I had to earn the right to play the game with him.

Dean had no concern for getting caught as we lay there on the floor, looking out the window of the double doors that led to the patio. I could see his mother hanging clothes on the line, and with two baskets filled, she wasn't coming into the house anytime soon. I watched *The Price is Right* on the old floor-model TV, hoping that he would be finished soon so we could play the game. But he seemed to go on forever and I was getting bored.

Suddenly Dean hurried me to my feet and pushed me against the wall. He got behind me and started to grind on me with his clothes still on, like a dog in heat. He was much stronger than me, so I couldn't fight back. Then he pulled me into the bathroom, which was only two doors down from the living room where we laid on the floor. He asked me to take off my pants, but I wouldn't. Dean pulled his pants down and was just about to pull mine down, but his mom came into the house, slamming the screen door behind her. Dean hurried to fix himself up, scrambling like he was trying to find something, walking back and forth, and looking around the bathroom as he quickly fixed his clothes. I assumed he was trying to think of an excuse as to why we were in the bathroom together, but I'm not sure.

After a few seconds, which seemed like minutes, Dean tore out of the bathroom like a snake was behind him, leaving me tailing behind. Dean's mother caught a glimpse of him running into his room, which was directly across the hall from the bathroom. He ran into his room so fast that you could only see the dark color of his shirt and feet as he crossed the hall.

After closing the main door and walking past the kitchen, Dean's mother found me standing by the bathroom door. She looked at me and asked, "What the hell were y'all doing?" She had that mother look on her face that scared me silly and unable to say a word! She had one hand on her hips, with the empty basket on the other hip. She opened

Dean's door, looked at him and said, "I know y'all asses were up to no good!"

Dean's mom made me go home and boy was she angry. As I left, I could hear a belt slapping Dean's flesh and him crying out, "No mama, no!" I later found out that he was on punishment for a few weeks and that he had to find someone his own age to play with, but it didn't end there.

A month or so later, Dean saw me outside and asked me to come over. There was a row of bushes that divided our yard from his, so I stuck my head through and asked if his mother was home. He told me she wasn't and that we were going to play a game. I declined, but he said it would be fun and that his cousin would play with us. His cousin was a chubby kid, about two years older than I was, light skinned and short.

After seeing Dean's cousin, I figured it would be okay. We walked to the side of the house, where Dean's grandfather was banished to smoke cigarettes. We sat on a burgundy bench across from the dumpster and talked about stuff. Then Dean decided that he wanted to smoke an old cigarette that he had found on the ground. He picked up the cigarette, straightened out the stub that had been stepped on, pulled out a lighter and put the cigarette up to his lips. When he tried to inhale the smoke, he looked like he was going to die. He coughed so hard that saliva poured out of his mouth as his hands reached for his chest. He took in some air, then suddenly, he flung forward and bent over like he'd been punched in the stomach. He coughed for a minute or so, until he was able to breathe again and regain his composure.

Dean's cousin picked up the cigarette and attempted to smoke it and practically did the same thing. I had often seen my stepfather smoking, so I blurted out, "Let me show you how it's done!" I had never smoked anything a day in my life until then, so I wasn't sure what I was about to show them, but I had already opened my big mouth, so I had to make good on it.

Dean's cousin handed me another newly straightened cigarette and I took a puff or a 'tote' as my mom would say. I inhaled, and the smoke filled my lungs. I instantly felt the nicotine coursing through my veins and suddenly, I felt cool, like I was the man. I blew the smoke out in a calm and steady stream and they looked at me in awe.

They asked in excitement, "How did you do that?"

I said, "It was easy. All you got to do is …" With my swag turned on high, I started to instruct them on the ways of a smoker as we picked up several cigarette butts and started to inhale. After we had gotten high on nicotine for a couple hours, Dean had another bright idea! He wanted to do a threesome between me, him and his cousin. This was to be conducted right there on the bench.

Dean proceeded to tell us how I was going to be on the bottom, his cousin was going to get on top of me and he was going to be on top of his cousin. I said, "You mean with our pants on?"

Dean said, "With our pants down and enter each other." I said that I didn't want to do it and they started teasing me, saying I was scared and that I was a punk. Then they said I could get on top next, as if that would make me feel better.

I continued to disagree with the idea, but they picked on me so much because of it, calling me names, saying I couldn't come back over anymore if I didn't do it, so I gave in. By this time, I was nine years old and everyone in school was calling me names and picking on me daily. The last thing I wanted was to be picked on and ridiculed by my peers at home. The kids in school didn't want to be friends with me because they were afraid of getting picked on if they hung out with me, and that was hard enough. I didn't want the guy that was supposed to be my best friend to stop wanting to be my friend too.

We were beside Dean's house on a bench and the next-door neighbor's house was right there. All anyone had to do was look out their window and they could see the trinity of young sinners doing ungodly deeds in their vicinity. I imagined that since Dean was not allowed to play with me anymore that he had turned to his cousin and went all the way with him; just like he tried to do me in the bathroom that day. Dean's cousin seemed to be very comfortable with the idea of being penetrated, but I wasn't. Even though I had agreed to it, once Dean's cousin got on top of me, I told them I didn't want to do it anymore. They weren't listening to me and kept trying to do their business. I started to rock from side to side to get Dean's cousin off me, but he held on like he was riding a horse or something.

Dean hopped on top of his cousin in a hurry and tried to go in him. I told them that I was being squished; that I couldn't breathe; that my stomach was hurting. Nothing would make them stop. I'm not sure if Dean had already entered his cousin, but all I know is that he was pumping away.

Meanwhile, I was starting to cry because they wouldn't let me free. Dean's cousin kept trying to put his penis in my butt, so I squirmed even harder to distort his aim and shake them off me. I remembered the P. E. class that I hated with a passion and how they would make us do those god-awful pushups, which I really couldn't do until that day. I treated the surface of that bench like it was a bad fart and pushed away from it with everything I had. I rocked the boat just enough to throw Dean off, but he hopped back on to his cousin's booty fast and started pumping again. As he hopped back up there, he pushed me flat on the bench, knocking the wind out of me. Now I was really in trouble because I couldn't catch my breath. I was crying and getting weaker from trying to push them off me. I could no longer squirm and just laid there trying to breathe.

Just when things were about to get bad and Dean's cousin was about to go for the goal, my sister started calling for me as she came around the front yard. Dean and his cousin jumped off me, pulled up their clothes and sat on the bench like nothing was wrong. I ran and hid behind the dumpster, curled up in a ball and continued crying. My sister kept calling for me, but I didn't answer. She saw Dean sitting there on the bench and asked them whether they had seen me, but they said nothing.

She heard me crying in the corner by the dumpster and asked, "What's wrong?"

I looked at her and said, "Nothing." But when I looked into her face I started crying even harder. My sister asked them what they had done to me, but they denied having anything to do with my tears, so she grabbed my hand and led me home. When I walked into my house, my mom was waiting on me and asked me what was wrong. They whispered about something that I couldn't hear. My mom asked me if Dean and his cousin did anything to me, but instead of saying yes, I burst into tears and wept like a newborn baby. I denied that anything had happened that day.

My feelings and my pride were hurt, and I realized that Dean wasn't my friend. I thought I would get in trouble if I told what happened and I didn't like whippings at all because my mother knew how to cut some butt. Instead of me getting in trouble, my mother sent me upstairs to my room and I was never allowed back over to Dean's house again.

I'm sure someone probably called my mom and told her what the boys were trying to do to me on the side of the house. I mean they were literally trying to rape me in broad daylight and I was screaming for them to get off me. They were in so much heat that they weren't even thinking about the consequences of their actions.

A few months after that situation, we had to move. I always thought it was my fault that we had to move, but my mother told me later that she didn't want us growing up in the hood anymore and the housing authority required us to vacate the premises. Mom moved us to a middle-class neighborhood in Forest Acres and things seemed like they were getting better the first year we were there, until I saw David again.

CHAPTER 7

He Came In

I was now thirteen years old and my life had been filled with ups and downs. Even though we had moved away from Burnswood, we still lived rather hood and were still poor according to society's standards, and ours for that matter. We still didn't have everything we needed, and because Mom wanted to move us out of the hood, it took more resources to maintain the home we were renting. The housing authority didn't cover the $800 a month rent that the landlord required, so my mom had to kick out an extra $200 to stay there, but it was worth it. The neighborhood was nice and multi-ethnic.

We had to walk or ride our bikes about a half mile down the road to find some kids of our own complexion and even then, they weren't the type of friends I was used to having. We had never really lived in the same quarters as white folk, so my mom would always tell us not to make too much noise in the backyard while we were playing. She didn't want the neighbors to complain about us living there.

She didn't want us to be 'niggers', as she would say. She didn't want her 'white neighbors' to complain about her 'black kids', to her white landlord. My mom didn't have too many parties or card games like we did in the hood. We couldn't play our music too loud and draw too much attention, because our house was on the corner and we could easily be noticed.

For the first year we couldn't play in the front yard a lot because my mom didn't want us to be noticed and cause too much trouble. I thought it was funny when the neighbors came out the door and greeted my mom because she would put on her proper voice to speak back to them; she was normally a country sap sucker! But she put on her 'white girl' voice when she talked to a white person. Listening to her enunciate and pronounce words that she wouldn't normally say correctly was so funny!

I will never forget my mother trying to tell someone that she needed to put socks on her feet, and her country roots came out. She said, "I need to put some socks on my foots!" But around white folk, you couldn't tell my mom that she wasn't proper. She would hold her head high as she talked, walk with her back straight, looking all proud saying yes ma'am and no sir! I guess she just wanted to keep the little she had and didn't want us to mess up the hard work it took to get us to that place. My mother taught us to be adaptable; be what they needed you to be, so you can get the results you want, and that is just what she did.

We never really had any trouble out of the people in the neighborhood. It was the kind of place that you can leave your front door open for hours and not have to worry about someone running in. It was the type of place where they had sidewalks, and people jogged up and down the street all day, walked dogs, rode bikes and skateboarded. It was a peaceful place. My mother felt comfortable leaving me and my little brother at home until she got back, but one day when I was home alone, I got an unexpected visitor.

Knock! Knock! Knock! I went to the door and asked, "Who is it?"

"It's David," came the reply, as if I knew he was coming. I opened the door because I thought it was someone else my sister had been talking to, but it wasn't who I thought it was and the door was already open. I stood there staring at his face, gazing so hard I seemed to look straight through him. David asked if my brother John was home, but as soon as he opened his mouth, flashes of the childhood I had forgotten came flooding back like a dam bursting on an unsuspecting town. So many emotions came over me at once. I wasn't sure what to do or what to think. I became so confused that I lost all sense of judgment and reason.

David kept talking, asking me questions about John I suppose, as I stood there staring off into space. His words became faint whispers of an unrecognizable dialect that I was supposed to understand but couldn't. Questions presented themselves like an army of soldiers standing on the front line, guns thrown over their shoulders, waiting for the sound of a battle horn. I must have been in a daze too long, because he asked me again, "Is your brother home?"

"No," I replied.

He said, "May I come in and leave him my number?"

I don't exactly know why I thought it was a good idea for me to say yes, but I did. I told him to wait in the den area while I got some paper.

He looked at me with those eyes; those molesting eyes and said, "My! My! My! Quanjay, you've sure grown up, um hmm!"

As he said those words, he looked up at me as if he was remembering what he had done to me and how he didn't get to finish doing all that he intended to do. As if the question had just come to him, he stepped forward, with his head cocked to the side and asked me how old I was now, but I didn't respond.

A bitter anger suddenly came over me, wrapped in fear and discomfort, encased in aggression and rage! With the intent of killing him, I lured him into the den area and asked him to have a seat while I found paper and a pencil. I didn't really have any intent on getting paper and a pencil; I intended on getting rid of him once and for all. He was never going to do to another kid what he had done to me.

I went into the kitchen and rattled the drawers and cabinets like I was looking for something. I grabbed the biggest knife that I could find and tiptoed out of the kitchen. I stood outside the den, next to the entrance, with my back against the wall. I stood there for a minute as he talked about this and that, talking in an elevated voice because he thought I was in another room; unsuspecting of my real intentions, not knowing I was so close.

As he talked, all I heard him saying was, "Whomp! Whomp! Whomp!" like the Charlie Brown characters do when someone is talking, and they zone out. I was so gone in my thoughts of murder that David startled me when he screamed, "What's taking so long?"

I moved away from the door slowly, then ran further down the hall before saying, "Nothing, I'm coming!" I wanted him to think that I was still in the kitchen, instead of standing against the wall, outside the doorway with a knife.

After I had told him that I wasn't doing anything, I tiptoed back to my ambush spot and began to pep-talk myself into what I was about to do. The time had finally come. This was it! The moment that I would get my revenge. I tried to play out the scenario in my head and planned how I was going to stab him to death without getting killed in the process. I knew he was sitting down when I had left him, so I figured that I could just turn the corner fast, catch him off guard and get one good stab off before he even realized what had happened. Then I would stab him a few more times and say that it was self-defense, because he had tried to rape me again.

With a foolproof plan to kill, I turned the corner fast with the knife in my hand, the way I had conjured up in my head. When I looked, he was standing up looking at pictures, with his back towards me. When he heard me turn the corner, he started to turn around, so I quickly put the knife behind my back just as he started to turn in my direction. David had already seen the knife before I could completely hide it and I thought we were about to fight.

He looked down at me and said, "I think I should just go." I said okay and allowed him to walk in front of me. Still holding the knife firmly in my hand, behind my back, I walked him to the front door. He opened the door and went out with his head hanging down, as if he had started to feel bad about what he had done to me. But it was already too late. I was angry, mad, frustrated, confused, had no trust and I wanted revenge. I wanted to kill him. I wanted to take out all my negative emotions on him at one time and feel better about him being gone from this world.

David stepped outside the door and started to turn around to say something to me, but I slammed the door in his face before he could utter a word. I looked out the peephole at him to see his response to the door being slammed in his face. He stood there gazing at the door for a few seconds, with a sad look on his face before turning around to walk down the steps.

After he left the sight of the peephole, I ran into the den and squatted in a corner by the side of our couch. The space had just enough room between it and the wall for me to squeeze into. With the knife still in my hand, I cried. I had forgotten about what had happened to me until he showed up at my door. I had forgotten about what David and Dean had done, but after he showed up at my door, everything came back to me in vivid HD quality and it stuck with me for a while. I remembered all the hurt, pain and everything that my childish mind had forgotten and forgave.

After David left, I became angry and violent. I wanted revenge for what had been done to me. I wanted back what had been taken away from me, but how? How would I get my manhood back? Even though no one knew about the molestation, I was still scared of anyone finding out what they had done to me, so I tried to prove to others that I wasn't gay by telling them about my sexual encounters; it was a defense mechanism. I tried to have as much sexual contact as I could, though most of what I said were lies.

Because of me being molested, I in turn wanted to take from others. By the time I reached the eighth grade, I had sexual experiences with female cousins, friends and myself. I was out of control. I couldn't get enough sex to satisfy what had now become an addiction. I used anything that would give me a sexual arousal. I humped teddy bears, pillows, the mattress and even my dog.

When I saw girls that I liked in school, who wouldn't give me the time of day, I thought about taking what I wanted from them. I figured that if someone had taken it from me, then I could just take what I wanted as well. Since nothing bad happened to them consequently, then I wouldn't get in trouble either. I thought these things, but I am so thankful that I never acted on my thoughts; however, the fact that it crossed my mind was scary enough.

I thought about raping girls every day for some reason. I had never known those thoughts until David came to visit and I didn't know what to do with them. My mind was in turmoil. I knew how it felt to have something taken away from me that wasn't given, so I wasn't exactly enthused about taking from someone else. I knew the betrayal and the dirty feeling it left me with after it was over. I knew the feeling of being alone; feeling like no one would understand and not wanting to tell anyone yet needing to tell someone. I felt like others would blame me for being raped, saying, "You were doing something you had no business doing in the first place." Even though that may have been true, the rapist still had no right to take from me and I had no right to take from others.

All those feelings caused an uncontrollable need to understand why the molesters did it. Why did they choose me? Were they stalking me or was it random? The thoughts I had caused me to want sex all day every day. I guess I was trying to understand them wanting to have sex with me and I in turn started wanting sex. I started using sex to make me feel better. Sex became my escape from the real world, and eventually I found porn. This became my addiction, and at such a young age, that was dangerous. I watched porn in all my free and spare time. I watched all kinds of porn. If it popped up in a little box randomly on the side of my screen, I looked at it or at least peeked at it.

Those who molest never stop to consider what will happen to their victims because of their actions. I often wonder, if they thought about it, would the image change their minds? If they saw the selfish, heartless, emotionally damaged person that they created, hiding behind flawless skin, beauty, things, money and achievements, would they have gone through with it? I wonder whether the molesters or rapists were raped as well or did they just up and decide that they would do it on their own? What caused them to be the way they are? Why didn't they get help or tell anyone that they were having those feelings and thoughts? Why, why, why did they pick my life to destroy? Why do I have to have this burden?

CHAPTER 8

Look What They Caused!

Not too long after David showed up at my door, I went from a joyful kid that liked to play outside to a frustrated, mad and violent kid. Because of the anger I had stored up from the years of constant nagging and people picking on me, I started to fight. I noticed that when I fought back, people would leave me alone. So, I fought harder and more often. I fought so much that people started knowing who I was for a different reason, other than me being ugly, black, fat and having man boobs. My defending became attacking. I became a bully. I fought people just to make an example and to show them that I was bad. I was no longer getting beat up, thanks to the months of slap boxing during the summer with my cousin, and it felt great!

Slap boxing with Detrick was like getting boxing lessons every day. I learned how to bob and weave, because if I didn't, I was going to get hit. Slap boxing wasn't really an option for me. Detrick would just walk up to me out the blue and start making a hissing noise like a snake, moving his hands all around, and next thing you know, 'pop!' You either got slapped or dodged the bullet. He would always get me with this uppercut slap to the chin and I hated it! So, after months of getting slapped, I learned how to dodge it, and before you know it, I knew how to fight. In just one summer I had learned everything I needed to know about winning a backyard fight, and I was good.

Even though I beat people up for picking on me, the bullying never stopped coming my way completely. The bullies that were bigger than me still picked on me and pushed me around. They constantly grabbed my chest and told me I had big titties. They told me how fat I was, and the girls said I was ugly. The boys didn't want to hang out with me and the girls didn't want to date me either. I had been turned down so many times in elementary and middle school that when I got to high school, all girls were sluts, whores, bitches and gold diggers.

I learned that both men and women wanted to use me and toss me away when they no longer needed me. Men will rape you and steal what's yours. Women will persuade you to do things you don't want to do and make you believe you did want to do it. I started to see that both smiled in your face around others and acted like they didn't do anything to hurt you.

Trust became a big issue for me. As the years passed I saw constant examples of who not to trust, why I couldn't trust them, and watched how they treated me and others. I started to learn people's ways. I started to understand that people treated certain people differently, according to their looks, how much they feared them, how much they respected them and how much they cared or loved them. I figured, if everybody just wanted to use me then I must do something to help myself, because no one else cared if I was hurting. My sisters had been leaving their young children with me against my will, so I never had a teenage life outside of school. I was always home watching kids or my younger brother, so I became bitter.

The lack of having my basic needs like food, water, lights, clothes, shoes, love and attention caused me to become self-sufficient. I got angrier that I had to look out for myself and that no one else cared enough to do it, besides me. I became a person that was willing to do whatever it took to protect myself.

My high school days were filled with mischief and mayhem. When a few young ladies expressed their interest, I would cut them down by calling them names. I thought they were only interested in me out of pity, because of the way people picked on me and called me names. I thought that no one could really truly like me!

I constantly got in trouble because I was trying to make a name for myself. I wanted people to know that I was 'the shit' and that I was, 'dat dude!' That's who I had become; a person who only cared about getting what he wanted. I developed a consciousness that didn't consider what others wanted from me and I started wanting to kill those who came against me.

I was 'hood'. All the principles I had learned about life were based on my experiences as a child. By the time a child is ten, you can just about determine that child's quality of life, if there is no intervention after that age. Even though my mom had attempted to move us out of the hood, I still preferred to hang out with those that I had grown accustomed to. I hung out around the drug dealers that played ball on the playground and hung out at the pool. It was comfortable. It was what I was used to. I didn't talk much, I just watched. I observed my environment and took in everything I could. I learned a lot. I found role models that really weren't good models, but in the hood, they were the best I could find.

There was this one kid named King. The only reason I really wanted to be like him was because of his fighting style. King fought like he was break dancing. He had this interesting way of moving his feet and body. He looked like he was gliding on air when he dodged a swing. I promise that it was like poetry in motion. King was also in a gang. It was one thing that I never wanted to do, but I became interested in it because he was in the gang.

I didn't have too many friends because I didn't trust men and I feared being gay. So, to avoid the possibility of being attracted to men, I stayed away from them as much as I could. I only befriended people if they had something I could use. I would pick their brains, learn their movements, attitudes and responses. King showed me how to move. I mimicked his boxing style and learned how to dodge a fist coming at my head. This meant that I would never get hit in the face again and I couldn't wait to test it out. King used to smoke Black & Mild's all the time, and because of trying one when he offered, I started smoking them too.

After I had gotten what I needed from King, we stopped hanging out. When guys wanted me to hang out with them, I was reminded of what Dean had done to me, calling himself my friend, and I wouldn't go to their houses. I only hung out with my cousins and their friends, whom I had no attachment to and could care less whether they liked me or not.

I learned a lot from watching other men as I sat on the sidelines of life and tried my best to be unnoticed out of fear of being picked on. I even maintained a C, D average in school to avoid being called a nerd. My whole life revolved around the fears that I had. It was a real fear; it was a clinching fear that never allowed me to make one friend until I was twenty-five years old!

I started wanting to kill people by the time I was a teenager and thought about it day and night. I wanted to kill those who had hurt me, those who bullied me and those who betrayed me. My mind became consumed with death. Even the thought of killing myself played like a recording in my mind. I rapped about killing people and it became an everyday, all day thought. I even wanted to get rid of those who picked on me. If they had something to say about the way I looked or what I wore, they had to die.

I attempted to lure a couple of kids from school. One at a time I invited them to the gym by my house. My hope was that they would come, and I would convince them to come to my house for some reason. We would walk through the woods right behind the gym to get there and I would kill them.

Though I tried many times, no one would meet me at the gym. I guess all those days of staring at people in class, with a crazy look on my face because I was imagining myself torturing them in some random way, kept them from coming. I can say now that I am glad that they were kept from me, because at that time I didn't care about anyone's life.

Since I couldn't kill the way I wanted to, I turned to what I knew best, sex. I was already addicted to porn and watching it every day. It was the only thing that made me feel good, and it seemed like the only reason to live at the time. Anytime I felt scared, alone, hurt or angry, I would turn to either food or masturbation.

During my freshman year in high school, I was told that I needed to have surgery on my leg, because of a deformity commonly known as bow legged. I was born with my left leg curved outward and it caused me to put too much pressure on one side of my body. Since I was so big, I was putting more pressure on my left leg than I needed to, causing it to swell with pain.

By this time, I was well over 400lbs. The summer after my freshman year in high school, I had the surgery on my leg. The doctor thought that scraping some of the growth tissue off one side of my leg would force it to correct itself. After having the operation, I couldn't return to school because I couldn't walk, so I was homeschooled, and my grades began to change. My tutor picked up my classwork and homework and took it back to the teachers when I was done. I started to make As and Bs in school because I didn't have the distractions that my classmates provided, and I didn't have to worry about being picked on all day.

Later that year I found out that my family had to move again because the homeowner went up on the rent. The housing authority wouldn't pay any more money than they were already paying, and Mom just couldn't afford to pay any more. We were already struggling and going months at a time without lights and water, so there was no way Mom could pay more.

My mom ended up finding a doublewide mobile home in Killian, SC that was on a pond, with a little bit of land to it. It was different to anything I had ever experienced. I liked the potential it had. I loved to fish, and when we went to look at the home, excitement filled me because I saw some big bass swimming along the edge of the water.

It took a few months for everything to go through with the home and we almost didn't get it at one time, but my mom kicked out enough money to get us there somehow. I swear I don't know how she pulled off some of the financial obligations she did, but I am glad that she was a hustler.

We moved into the doublewide and it was a very peaceful environment. We were literally living in the country now and I loved it! My next-door neighbors had chickens that crowed in the morning. Some neighbors had big gardens, growing corn, collard greens and other veggies, and others had flowers. We went from the hood, to the suburbs, to the country. I liked that good ole southern country living better than I liked living in the hood or the suburbs. Life in the country was much easier and much more peaceful. At any given time of the day I could escape my world by throwing a hook in the water and watching the fish tug on my line!

My mom was the queen of fishing. She would catch all the best fish, even when we went to the lake, and she would be the only one catching fish most of the time. Everyone else would pull out a baby or two, but she would pull out brim that were the size of a man's hand repeatedly; talk about good eating! When Mom put the fish in the bucket half-filled with water, she would say, "This will make a good sandwich right here!" Or she would point out which fish was personally hers to go with grits the next morning. Watching Mom would always make me smile, because she did funny stuff all the time.

When I asked her how she caught so many fish, she would say, "You have to hold your mouth right to catch fish boy!" I would throw my hook back in the water and try to hold my mouth a certain way to catch fish, trying out different mouth-holding techniques. Mom would watch me tooting my lips up, turning them sideways and making crazy faces, while trying to get a bite, and laugh at me!

One day Mom finally told me the secret mouth-hold technique to catching fish. She looked me square in the eyes, came up close to me, made her lips look like fish lips and moved her lips up and down. I fell out laughing! I laughed so hard that I couldn't breathe! It was the kind of laugh that made you cough and hold your stomach. You know the one that causes a silent pause for a few seconds and you feel as if you are about to die from laughing so hard.

Fishing around the pond was great, but now I had to go to a new school, but it was a better school. I enrolled at Ridgeview High with a new mind. I had seen my potential to make good grades and I was determined not to be a failure. Even though I had good intent, there were a few kids that saw an opportunity to take advantage of me because I was a new guy.

I was walking down the hall on the second day at the school, looking at my schedule, trying to figure out where to go. Then suddenly, a guy walked right up to me and acted like he was about to spit in my face. I responsively reared back to hit him, but just as my fist was beginning to make its way towards his face, he yelled, "I was just playing!"

I was able to stop myself from hitting him, but the momentum from the swing caused me to go forward. I found myself in his face. I whispered something to him like it was a scene from a mob movie. I told him, "Don't you ever do that again!" I turned away to walk off, only to find that everyone was looking at me as if I was Scarface. I found out that the guy I punked out was supposed to be a badass, and after that day I had become one too! My intentions of being good and different in a new school had gone out the window real fast and now I was a target. People started asking me to join their gangs constantly, but I didn't want to join.

If I was picked on, it came from the girls. Most of the guys were too scared to say anything because I would fight anybody. After slap boxing and beating a few of the school's prize fighters I hardly had any challengers in a fist fight, but I didn't want to fight anymore anyway.

Ridgeview was a different type of school than I was used to. It was a mixed school. There were blacks, whites, Hispanics, Indians, Asians and other cultures learning together. It was the first time that I had ever interacted with anyone from another culture, let alone someone from a completely different country. Everything I had been taught about other races had been eradicated in a few days; it was like I was in a different world. People from other cultures were friendly and they didn't hate me like I had been taught. Some of them respected me as a person and some of them didn't. It was interesting to experience something new for the first time, but it didn't cause me to change much. I continued to do what I was used to doing – fighting and striking fear into my peers. I lived two different lives in school. Some teachers knew me as a good student, but others saw me at my worst. Some students knew me as a good guy and some saw me as a terrorist.

I quickly learned that the type of women I was attracted to didn't like bad boys, they liked the good ones. I met an Asian-American girl named Cynthia that I started to like, but I didn't have the guts to tell her. One day I asked to play in her hair, and after that I was really hooked. She set off every fire that I had, and I wanted her to have my baby.

I wrote Cynthia a poem and she fell in love with me, and she walked down the hall on my arm that same day! Talk about happy and proud. People were talking and jealous. Suddenly, I had become a ladies' man, because I pulled the Asian girl

Cynthia changed how I looked at women and how I felt about dating outside of my race, but it didn't last long. What seemed like only a week after that day she walked with her hands clasped together with mine, she told me she was moving out of state. I wasn't sure how to feel. I was shocked and didn't want her to go, but there was nothing I could do about it. I was hurt that she was leaving, but I acted like I didn't care by brushing it off. I am sure that I made her feel unimportant, but she really was important to me.

I was in the library when she told me that she was leaving, and I acted as if I didn't care, though I was hurt, but after my response of, "Okay, goodbye," she walked out of the library looking hurt. I had gotten used to people leaving me, and not caring or moving on quickly was a way to protect myself. I sat there for a few seconds, scolding myself for being a jerk, then got up and ran out the door looking for her. I ran up and down the halls and outside, but she was gone. She came into my life and had been taken away just like that. I never got a chance to tell her how I felt and that I wanted to love her. I didn't get her number, her new address or anything. I really believed that her father didn't want her to date me, but I can't say for sure. All I know is that I beat myself up for years when it came to Cynthia, my Asian persuasion!

One thing is for sure, after losing Cynthia I never hesitated to tell a girl how I felt, even if it meant getting my feelings hurt, and I got them hurt a lot of times too, but at least they knew what I wanted and my intentions. I became a sweetheart after Cynthia. I started writing poetry a lot more and being kind to women, instead of treating them disrespectfully. The way Cynthia looked at me with compassion never left me; it was the first time someone looked at me with genuine love and care, but would it be the last?

CHAPTER 9

He Gave Me Hope

By the time I had reached my junior year of high school, I was becoming even more of a knucklehead. One teacher saw through all that anger, pain and disappointment. His name was Mr. Bee, my electronics teacher. He was very good at his job, but he was a bit clumsy and nerdy.

The kids used to pick on him because he had a habit of slobbering out of his mouth as he talked. It was kind of funny at first, but after about a week or so in class, I saw through all the clumsiness. Sometimes he would drop a marker or eraser, then look back at us while bending down to pick it up and say, "Sorry class" or "Excuse me!" I promise he looked like Steve Urkel from *Family Matters*!

While Mr. Bee was talking about resistors or something, spit would trickle down either side of his lips. Sometimes he would catch it, sometimes he wouldn't. When he tried to catch his spit, it made it even funnier! I mean the class would go into an uproar of laughter, students falling out of chairs and banging on desks.

The students picked on him constantly. One day I got tired of it and told the class to chill out because I was trying to learn, and they listened to me. It shocked me that they shut up so fast, but I couldn't show that I was shocked. I maintained a mean mug for a few minutes, while looking around the class, to signify who the boss was.

Mr. Bee was really a great teacher and I loved learning about electrical engineering the way he taught it. He was the man that really caused me to desire something greater than my current circumstances. I used to walk down the hall and shout a phrase that the guys liked to say for absolutely no reason. It went like this, "Skeeeeeyooouuu!" I would try to be the one who said it the loudest, held it the longest and said it the deepest! It was purely to attract attention and show defiance for authority. It caused other kids to fear us, to respect us and it let teachers know that we ran this, and they needed to play by our rules. At least that's why I did it. Maybe others did it just for the attention, but I was thinking about taking over.

One day Mr. Bee caught me acting a fool, using profane language in the halls, and called me into his classroom. I wasn't supposed to be in his class that period, but he wanted to have a few words with me anyway. He told me that he would give me a pass to class, and since I didn't want to go to my next period anyway, I took the opportunity. Mr. Bee sat down at his desk and started tinkering with a circuit board. He was telling me that I was different from the rest of the knuckleheads that roamed the halls. He told me that I had potential and that I didn't have to be like the rest of them, that I could do something different.

He saw that I was intelligent and that I was trying to be ignorant so that I could fit in. Mr. Bee talked to me about how great men and women died so that I could have the opportunity to get an education. He briefly shared his upbringing with me and told me that I should take advantage of my education and be all I could be.

He continued to bestow affirmations upon me like I was king or something, then smoothly ended the conversation by talking about the circuit board that he was tinkering with the whole time. "Do you know what a resistor does?"

"No," I said.

Mr. Bee looked up at me and said, "It's a device used to control the flow of electricity in a circuit." He told me that an electrical current with no resistor could fry a circuit because too much electricity can flow through unregulated. Then he looked at me with those bug-like, beady eyes, and his head was tilted down as he looked through the top of his glasses. He proceeded to tell me about all the different parts that controlled the flow of electricity and gave power to the circuit board.

I didn't realize it, but he was teaching me how to route all the negative energy from my experiences, filter them out and turn them into something positive. Whether Mr. Bee intended for me to one day have an awesome revelation, I don't know. Maybe he knew that one day that seed of wisdom was going to blossom into a mighty tree and bear fruit, and maybe he didn't, but I am thankful that he took the time to impart such wisdom in my life.

After that day I started to change my outlook about the future. I started to realize that I could be great; that I could go to college and get a scholarship. Before Mr. Bee had talked to me, I never dreamed of going to college because I knew that my family couldn't afford it, and no one talked to me about scholarships, grants and getting loans.

No one had told me that I could be whatever I wanted to be. No man had ever talked to me about my future and told me that I had potential, but after that day I instantly became an A, B student again. I no longer cared about the opinions of other people and what they thought about me, I just wanted to be the best or at least in the top 3%. Mr. Bee kept encouraging me to do better all that year and I banged out my junior year with the highest grades I had ever made in school since the second grade!

******

It seemed like school had come and gone, now it was summer. My summer went by the same as usual, going to the gym to play basketball, smoking stuff I didn't have any business smoking, and cutting grass, mostly for money.

When I went back to Ridgeview after the summer break for my last year of high school, Mr. Bee was gone. I am not sure what happened to him, but my new electronics teacher was not who I looked for when I signed up for the class. I got through the class, but it just wasn't the same; I didn't enjoy electronics much after that, but I still wanted to pursue it.

I remembered everything that Mr. Bee told me, and I did well that year too. I graduated on time and high school was finally over. I was free from so many of the kids who made my life a living hell every day and I never had to see them again.

College was in my future. I chose DeVry because I wanted to be like Mr. Bee. I was excited about going to DeVry so that I could major in electrical engineering, so I applied to the college. A DeVry representative came to my house during my senior year of high school and talked with my mom, who seemed worried because she didn't have any money for college saved up for me. But after the rep had told her about loans and grants, she relaxed and felt better.

Everything was in motion, I was set to go to college and I was happy, but just before I was going to leave SC and go to GA for college, I experienced another stumbling block. I went back to the doctor who had performed the surgery on my knee the first time and he told me that the surgery didn't work too well. He told me that he needed to do another surgery, but this one would be different to the other. He advised me that if I didn't get the surgery done, I might be in a wheelchair by my thirties. So, I had a choice to make, either get the surgery or go to college.

After much deliberation and pressure from others, I chose to go with the surgery. I was still under eighteen and Medicaid would pay for the surgery, so it was now or never. No one advised me that I could have afforded to have the surgery one day; they didn't give me any other options. My mother or stepfather didn't have me on their job insurance and my real dad never put me on his insurance, so my mother thought that this would be the best option for me to have a promising future.

The surgery involved the breaking of my left knee and ankle. The doctor hoped to turn my leg and ankle inward so that the bone would be reformed in the right position. I decided to go through with the surgery and the prep work began. I needed to lose as much weight as I could before the surgery, so I lost a grand total of twenty pounds.

On the day of the surgery, I was afraid that I was going to die. I said my goodbyes like I would never see my mom and family again. They put the mask on me and told me to start counting backwards from ten to zero, but I only remember getting to seven.

During the recovery time, months after the surgery, I had turned eighteen and Medicaid refused to pay for any rehabilitation. With a broken leg and ankle, I could not walk. I had a big, cast iron brace on my leg, with wires from my knee to my ankle, going through my leg, holding my bones in place. I felt paralyzed. I felt as if I would never walk again.

I didn't have anyone to really care for me the way I needed to be cared for. I had to do a lot of things on my own. No one wanted to take care of a grown man in constant pain, I guess, so I started to feel sorry for myself and began feeling like a burden. It was hard for my mom to help me the way I needed it and go about her daily tasks, so I started trying to do everything on my own.

It was hard, real hard! I had gotten so low and was very depressed. I wanted to kill myself, so I took a bunch of pain pills and I lay in the bed; I lay there waiting to die. I really didn't want to die, but I figured that it was better than having this feeling and going through the pain. I started to get dizzy and passed out after taking the pills. I thought I was dying when I passed out because I was short of breath, but I woke up hours later with absolutely no pain in my knee. It had been the best sleep I'd gotten since I came home from the hospital. I'm not sure if I came close to death or not. All I know is that I slept a very long time.

It seemed as though I couldn't kill myself, so I started using food as my comfort again. I packed on a lot of weight, very fast! I'll never forget going to a family function for my grandmother's birthday and my mom had to buy me this ugly short pant set that was the only size they had in her budget. It was a size 6x large, the biggest size I had ever gotten, and I was miserable sitting in that restaurant.

It seemed as though there was a big elephant in the room, and guess who it was? It felt like my family was talking right over me. When it was time for me to order, it was almost like the restaurant went quiet and waited for me to order half of the menu. To show them that they were wrong, I ordered one small burger that I got mad at after I was done eating because I was still hungry.

Months went by and I got bigger. It was time for the cast iron brace to come off my leg and I was happy. Now I would be left to learn how to walk on my own. The doctor had pity on me and my situation and gave me enough medical supplies to continue treating the leaking wounds myself, and I appreciated that.

The offer for DeVry had expired and classes were now full. Even if I wanted to go, I would need to learn how to walk first. During the time of my healing I had attempted suicide by medication pills and tried to slit my wrist, but for some reason that razor wouldn't go through my skin, even though it cut right through a piece of paper. Since I didn't want to go jump off a building, I ate my problems away and got up to over 500lbs. I remember getting on a scale at Walmart, the one that requires a quarter and it read 565lbs. This was the heaviest I had ever been. Walking around on a walker and being so overweight was embarrassing and I didn't want to go anywhere anymore, but I continued to gain weight after that.

It was hard learning how to walk after becoming so heavy. After failing at committing suicide, I found inspiration in my nieces and nephew, who gave me a reason to live. I always made them laugh and would scare them by chasing them around the house. They have these wild stories of things I did to them when they were little. They say that I chased them around the house with a knife, acting like I was going to kill them, foaming out the mouth and whatnot. One of them said that I was acting like I was non-responsive, then got up possessed by some creature with a deep voice. While I don't recall any of that, it's possible that I may have scared them a time or two when they were acting up and getting on my nerves.

It took me a year to teach myself how to walk again and it took me another year and a half just to learn how to run. No one helped me to walk and I often had to crawl so that I could make it to the bathroom. I even went on myself a couple of times trying to make it to the toilet, but I never gave up, I kept on trying. I thought about what Mr. Bee had said to me, and I wiped my tears and kept trying.

CHAPTER 10

They Made Me a Criminal

Everyone passed me by! My brothers left me at the house while they had fun and my cousins did the same. My sisters left their kids with me against my will as they had always done and there seemed to be nothing I could do about it. No matter how much I complained, fussed and cursed, they still did what they wanted to do.

By the time I started learning how to walk, I had developed some sort of nerve pain in my back. Every time I stood up straight, my right leg would suddenly start to go completely numb after about thirty seconds. I timed it because I was trying to cure myself, and I had to know just how much time I had to adjust without causing too much pain.

I would bend over backwards on the arm of my mother's wooden chair and attempt to crack my back or reposition my disc. I tried everything I could find online or read in a book. Then one day I read something that talked about pressure being on the disc and causing inflammation and how being overweight can cause that pressure. Well, sure enough, after learning that I lost about 30 or 40lbs, and the nerve pain went away. After my nerve pain went away, I could walk normally again.

When I was eighteen years old my sister had gotten a new car, and, after some begging, she gave me her old car, which was a 1991 Ford Escort that had transmission issues and it wouldn't start. I recalled all the years my stepfather forced me to help him with his cars and I got a mechanics book and learned how to fix the car myself.

I appreciated the car because it allowed me to get out the house and finally be my own man. I quit the McDonald's job I had and got a job selling 'Indoor Air Quality Systems' and it was on from there! I worked hard and started to make my own money. I was now free to do what I wanted to do, when I wanted to do it, and that is just what I did.

I started selling drugs because I saw others doing it and getting paid, so I figured I could do the same and didn't have to work so hard. I was tired of working at fast food joints and doing the sales position, which was commission only, so I got a job as a pizza delivery driver and started my plan.

My plan was to deliver pizza and drugs at the same time. It was a good cover because when I had stacks of money, it looked like tips. When I wanted to deliver my drugs, I put them in a breadstick box and took it into the buyer's house. I could take money in public and it looked like I was delivering pizza to someone.

My little plan worked for years, as I sold drugs and never got caught. I made a couple grand a week, nothing big, as I didn't want to draw any attention to myself. I was good at hiding in the shadows. My alias was, 'JYD tha GHOST'. No one really knew how much drugs I was selling; all they knew is that I had money all the time. I sold to regular people and hood people. I had a system; I had a way of doing things and I didn't allow anyone to get in the way of that, because I didn't plan on going to jail.

I was once told that a real G doesn't go to jail, others go to jail for them. I learned that I had two options – get a crew willing to take the fall for me or to think before I made decisions, especially since I had already seen what got others caught up. So, I did the opposite of what got others caught. I didn't have friends I hustled with. I didn't let women know my business. I made friends with cops because I delivered pizza to their houses, extra cheese here, box of breadsticks there, a little free pizza, some free wings and I was in the game. I learned to provide a need so that I could get what I wanted. That's what everyone did to me anyway, so I did it to others.

I remember getting pulled over once for speeding. I had a few pounds in the back of the car and I knew I smelled like weed. The cop threw his lights on when I passed him and circled around like a whip cutting the corner. I knew I was in trouble. I sat up straight, put on my educated voice, and prepared myself to talk my way out of this one.

When the cop came to the window, it was a guy that I delivered pizza to, so it was easier than I thought. I told him I was just trying to get the pizza to the house hot, like I did his pizza, and he said, "And I appreciate that. Tell you what Mr. Jones, go on and slow it down just a tad, keep under ten."

I said, "Yes sir," and got on through, feeling like I was the man. I was thankful that he didn't pull me out of the car because he smelled the weed.

I sold drugs and delivered pizza in my '89 Champaign Cadillac Deville and rode around looking clean doing either one. I ran from police in the 'Lac, engine wide open, cutting corners and floating down the road driving 85mph and above. I fought, shot guns and tried to do everything in secret. I didn't go brag about it to the boys, because people talked, and I learned from a child that you can't trust anyone, not even your closest friends.

One cousin taught me how to cook dope and another one taught me how to sell it. I had weed under control, I could eyeball a pound or a couple of ounces and be on the head. But selling dope brought a different type of customer and a different type of attention than selling weed.

I learned quickly that crackheads and cocaine users snitch often. It wasn't even a week from when I had started selling dope that I got a call from jack boys trying to see what I could get. My phone rang, and I answered it and said, "Yo!"

The guy on the other line said, "Yo, what up tho, I want to get eight ball from ya!"

I said, "Who dis?" I didn't recognize the number and I had trained everybody that I sold to on a regular basis how to talk to me on the phone, and this was not the way. I said, "I don't know what you talking bout homie. You got the wrong number."

He replied, "Nah, I got the right number, how much can you get? I want the whole thang."

I already knew they were trying to set me up, so I hung up the phone. I received calls like that, asking for weight, from people I didn't know for another week, then they suddenly stopped calling. I started getting paranoid. I was getting pulled over randomly when I wasn't speeding or doing anything crazy. Then I learned that because I had gotten a car that looked like someone else's, who was a hot boy and lived around the corner from me, they thought I was him.

I had brought a white Grand Marquis and both of us had a white Grand Marquis. We both brought weight from the same guy and the cops started following me, so I had to be extra careful. I noticed other cars following me and realized why a person needed a team in the dope game, but I didn't want a team. I didn't trust anyone, and even though I had been asked to join gangs by members of the Crips, I didn't want to be a part of something that told me what to do, when to do it, and how to do it.

I didn't have the Grand Marquis too long after that. The heat came down on me too hard, with the police constantly pulling me over. I stopped selling dope and went back to selling weed. I could make the money and didn't have to worry about all the attention, but I was on the radar now and I didn't like it. I kept doing my thang, getting smarter, watching more, telling others how to do it, what to do, where to do it. I started becoming good at being a criminal. Stealing, jacking on my own and with a cousin, doing all the things that criminals do.

I got drunk daily, smoked weed, sold weed and rapped about it all. One day while writing a rap, I ran out of blunts, so I went to the store. It was something about that day. There was a little sunshine out, but the breeze and the temperature were just right. I rode with the windows down and the music was turned off while on the way to the store. I saw a girl, who had thick thighs and a nice booty, as I pulled into the parking lot and I thought about talking to her, but I changed my mind, which was unusual, because I normally tried to get every girl that looked my way. The bell on the top of the door at the convenience store rang as I entered. I walked to the fridge to grab a drink and walked to the counter.

"Let me get two green leaf Dutch Masters and your cheapest lighter. Oh yeah, and that two eleven right there is mine too!" I reached into my pocket to hand the clerk some money, pulling the rubber band off the stack of bills I had in my hand. I flipped through them until I got to a five, handed it to her, and then told her to keep the change. I grabbed my bag, dapped my homie up that came into the store, walked outside and got into my '89 Champagne Cadillac Deville. The seats were so far back that I had to lean to the side just to see as I drove. I rode with my left hand on the top of the wheel and my elbow resting on the center console, music bumping loud, listening to some beats that I'd made, freestyling about anything I thought of.

With one hand still on the wheel, I reached for the ounce of weed that I had stashed in the glove compartment and started to break up enough buds to fill one of the blunts I picked up from the store. By the time I got home, I was ready to roll up! I got out of the car and walked into the bricked-in, doublewide trailer on a pond that we were renting. I walked into the room, turned on some Bob Marley and listened to him sing 'No Woman No Cry' until I got settled in and ready to twist up!

I grabbed the book that I used to roll weed on and prepared myself for the masterpiece I was about to create. With my two thumbnails, I split the Dutch down the middle and threw the guts in the ashtray. I licked the edges of the blunt for handling purposes, then sprinkled weed down its center. Looking like a professional cigar maker, I tightly rolled the blunt to keep everything in, yet loose enough to smoke evenly without over-burning. I saturated the outside of the blunt with saliva to create a seal during the drying process.

I used a lighter to heat the outside of the blunt just long enough to dry it and activate the seal, preventing it from unraveling as I smoked. The moment of truth had arrived. Flick! Flick! I put the flame to the tip of the blunt as I held the other end with the edge of my lips. I closely observed the Dutch, taking it out of my mouth, putting it back in again, while still holding the lighter's flame to the tip of it.

I cautiously took in the first wave of smoke as I laid my head back on the bed. But this high was different; this high was not like the rest. This time I thought about why I was getting high in the first place. What caused me to want to get high? Usually someone else would ask me why I smoke weed, but this time I asked myself the question. Why *did* I smoke so much anyway? I took a few more hard hits and I heard a voice say, "You are running from something!" So, I asked the voice, "What am I running from?"

CHAPTER 11

I Came Down

I had been thinking about my childhood years and its effects for months now. I smoked and thought, smoked and thought. Weed had become my therapist. It allowed me to escape my current problems long enough to focus on how they began in the first place. I smoked so much that I couldn't get high anymore. The high would only last for about ten minutes, no matter how many blunts I smoked. I had, in a sense, gone back in time, thinking about situations and circumstances and how they made me feel.

After I came down off my constant high and allowed my mind to breathe for a few days, I was left with all the stuff I remembered from my childhood. All the things that I had forgotten; all the hurt that was replaced with anger; all of it had now been explained. It was a defining moment. When you look back at yourself and realize that the mirror of your life is a distorted truth of who you really are and could become, it can change you. This ascertainable truth to the consequences of my self-righteous actions had proven to be a worthy foe. How can a man fight himself and claim victory?

I realized, more than anyone could ever understand, that my future depended on the felicitous administration of my present and the amnesty of my past. Those few months of getting high and thinking about my past as it related to my present caused me to desire a change. I started to realize why I was getting high and drunk in the first place. I was trying to run from my past and escape my present circumstances. Circumstances that had been molded and shaped by the hurt of my past.

Everything that I was going through was all because of what I had been through. I became bound to events that I couldn't change; events that I blamed myself for, even if there was no way that I could have stopped them from happening. I had to face the fact that my choices had been manipulated by the many situations that in a sense molested my mind.

I was on a new journey now. I felt like I was looking through new eyes, breathing through new lungs, hearing in a different language. I realized that pain had taken away some valuable years and that I had to find a way to get them back somehow.

I began to recall my days in college and the psychology courses that I took. I started to dive into the roots of my problems, asking myself questions, hoping to get a valuable answer. I started to learn and grow by leaps and bounds. My entire life started to change right before my very eyes. I started paying attention to every action and every word. I wondered why I did this and why I did that. "Who, what, when, where, why, how and if?" were the questions that I asked daily. I started to understand strongholds and principles as I learned how my past experiences affected me.

Strongly Held Principles

A stronghold is something that is established to keep people out; a place that is fortified and can be easily defended. After learning about strongholds, I started to understand the things that caused me so much trouble, like the animal that came out of me when I was backed into a corner. That animal was born the moment I was denied freedom under that bed. Feeling trapped in any way caused me to defend myself uncontrollably, no matter the person or situation. Wanting to be free of whatever was bothering me or keeping me bound caused me to lash out or run to a safe place.

I realized that I was responding out of the emotion of my past and not my present. My bishop, Duane Greene, always says, "If you can remember the place of a bee sting, you haven't forgotten the pain of it." Some people know they have been stung by a bee, but they can't identify the place of the sting, while others that have been stung remember the exact place of the sting, even if it is ten, fifteen or twenty years later. Some people forget the pain, while others hold on to it and fear it. Those who hold on to it never forgave the first bee that stung them!

Just like the bee sting, we often remember the pain in our lives. Sometimes we can, and sometimes we can't, pinpoint the pain, yet we know that we've experienced it. You must forgive the first bee to accept and be in the presence of the next bee that flies by you, otherwise you might run out of your socks trying to get away from the first bee that stung you, not the bee that just flew by you!

There are those who were stung years ago, when they were children, and the experience was so intense that they still remember the pain of the sting. Strongholds are often set up in our minds like pillars that we refer to in those situations anytime we're faced with anything that resembles them. If we aren't careful, our responses to our past can hurt our present.

There were many strongholds that took root in my mind. I didn't trust men and I responded violently to threats that weren't very serious and responded even worse to those that were. I didn't want to get undressed in front of guys, or women for that matter, for a long time. I didn't like to be alone, because being alone always led to trouble. I became a people pleaser. I became protective of anybody being taken advantage of. I was unsure of my sexual identity, preference or needs, but I wanted to be pleased constantly.

I became socially inadequate, uncomfortable in my own skin and even began to desire what had been done to me, wanting to take something from someone against their will, though I never gave in to those thoughts. I remember what it felt like to have something taken from me. I remember the pain that it caused me. Causing that pain in someone else was not going to work for me. Being so young and having those thoughts was very confusing.

At twelve years old, the results of those molesting's had disturbed the fabric of my mind and caused me to do things that I would not have done, had I not been molested. I learned that there was an alluring power behind taking something from someone. If I allowed the addiction of it to take hold, it could send me into a swirling echo of duplicated behavior; the victim could become the attacker.

I indulged in many sexual acts and behaviors because of the mind that was created from being molested. Those predators took my body, but they molested my mind. When I was lied to about the candy being under the bed and lured away, I felt betrayed. I felt like I had not gotten my fair share of what was due to me and that taught me one of a few lessons; never take what people say at face value. If you wanted me to believe it, you had to prove it.

Wanting proof for everything is not necessarily a good thing because it hurts your ability to have faith in or trust people. I didn't want to be lied to again, because falling victim to a lie got me hurt. This type of mindset can be a hindrance in relationships. I wanted people to believe me, but I didn't believe them. This stronghold made it seem as if I believed that I was right about everything and others were always wrong. People didn't know about my stronghold and I was also unaware of its effects until I started asking myself questions. Strongholds can turn into principles if they go unnoticed and unregulated.

A principle is defined as the first, or among the first, in importance or rank. In other words, if something happens, what is the first root you refer to that helps you respond to or solve problems and pertaining to a situation? The establishment of a stronghold in trust caused me to protect myself from being bamboozled or hoodwinked ever again and it seemed perfectly normal for me to do that.

I didn't see a problem with needing people to prove themselves to me. I needed to verify what I was being told. I needed to verify their actions, thoughts and even their loyalty, but because I trusted me, there was no need to verify the same things in myself. Because I needed proof, I sought to prove things to myself all the time, which meant that I became what most would call a know-it-all.

If anyone wanted me to prove my position in any way, I was ready to do so. If I said it, I was going to be able to back it up. Even if someone said I was cute, I wanted them to prove it. Having that mindset meant that I couldn't accept something good as being true without questioning whether the person said it because they wanted something from me. I was used to people using me and lying to me, so much so that, according to my mind, everyone wanted to use me.

This had a hard effect on my relationships. No one should have to prove everything to me. It was a burden to my friends, family and significant others. It started to make sense why my relationships would start off good, then get difficult. Those who once confided in me stopped talking to me or telling me their feelings. All of them would say I was hard to talk to, or they had found someone else to talk to, which in turn made me feel abandoned or not wanted/needed.

I couldn't understand why others didn't want to confide in me anymore, until I started to break down the 'why' of the results. I broke down the 'why' to its most minute fragment to see what caused it. I had a friend who told me about being raped by a guy who was supposed to be a reputable person in his community. She explained how it happened, and because she had lied to me before, I didn't believe her. I questioned her as though she had caused it, and, in a sense, I wanted her to prove that she had been raped.

I thought she wanted me to feel sorry for her because we weren't talking due to her past lies. I thought that it was her way of using a situation to lure me back into her life, and I was not going to be used or lied to again. Her pain didn't matter to me; however, mine did. Her consistent inability to tell me the truth had set up a stronghold in my mind that was only for her. I believed that she was incapable of telling the truth and I had to guard myself against her at all cost, no matter what she told me.

One stronghold led to another and another, until I found myself spiraling out of control. I should have given her a shoulder to cry on, because that's why she came to me in the first place, for comfort. But because I allowed those strongholds to take root, I made her feel guiltier than she felt before she called me, and I know that feeling; having something taken from you that you didn't give. I was supposed to understand because I knew what it felt like, and to comfort her based on that understanding, not condemn her.

There are many principles that have been established in my mind that started off as strongholds. They became a part of my core being, something I believed in and even taught to others through my thoughts and actions, whether they were right or wrong. Our principles can transfer and become other people's principles, this is called being a role model.

Role Model

I learned what it meant to be a role model; what it meant to hold the clay of life in your hands and witness the power of a blank canvas, ready for a caring heart to shape their future with loving words of endurance and perseverance. To teach them about faith and hope, trials and tribulations, battles lost, and wars won. That canvas you hold in your hands has the power to be the shape of hope. It has the power to be the model for love. It can be something great that the world has never seen before. It can create and make the world a little bit better, but it also has the same ability to make it worse.

What will you do with the creation you will help design? Will you just throw it away and remove yourself from responsibility because of your incapacity to care or love? Will you be a part of something you have created? Will you hold that creation in your hands, being responsible for its wellbeing and care for it with respect, the way that God cares for you?

Being a role model means that you have a role to play in shaping the future of whomever watches you act. Your life, your walk, is a movie; your words are the script. Whatever you say will be recorded by the eyes and ears of those who see you every day. Whatever you do will be replayed like a tape in the mind of whomever you inspire. What you inspire them to do is your responsibility.

If you are a role model, your life is a sequel. You are live on the set. Each new moment is more valuable than the other, because the new moments are the ones we remember first. The last moments are merely experiences that teach us how to rightfully make decisions in our future. Thus, if the past is a minute ago, use the next one to make a decision that will change a life, either yours or someone else's.

Right now, is all that is important; what you have going on today, this very hour, this minute, right at this present second. This is what matters because no one can change yesterday. Yesterday has forgiven itself and moved on to tomorrow, but you are stuck in a place where time doesn't matter, and you are blind to its healing power. A place where you still hear the screams of your youth and the cries of your heart being broken. A place where you feel the pain of your past like fresh paper cuts on your flesh. But if you remain there, time will not cease, and life will pass you by. Opportunities will knock, and your decisions, which are based on how you overcame your past, will determine whether you are able to answer the door to your future. If you remain in a dark place, your light will never shine and someone who is waiting on you to guide them won't be able to move. They will become trapped in darkness.

Imagine that you are blind, and you have a guide leading you with a flashlight in his hand; he leads you but doesn't turn on the light to see a clear path. Even though he guides you and can see, he remains in darkness, because he refuses to use the flashlight thinking that he can do it without help, but he is just as blind as you are, only he chooses to be. Because you are blind, you don't know if he can see. You assume that the one leading you is capable of vision, so you follow that person willingly, but if you don't know what sight is, how can you determine whether someone else is blind?

My bishop Duane Greene has a saying, "Never let a naked man sell you clothes!" How can someone tell you how to get out of something they've never been in or gotten out of? If you really don't understand or lack the knowledge of how to use the light, stop pretending to be a guide and get back there with the blind until you understand how to see. What I'm saying is that even role models need role models.

During my time of selling drugs, I influenced young men who saw me living the life they wanted to live, doing the things they wanted to do. I pulled out rolls of money from every pocket and always had women coming by the house, and other women wanted me as well. I did what I wanted, went where I wanted and ate what I wanted, I had options or choices. People will kill for the ability to have options, the right to choose what they want.

One day I saw a young man that used to come to the music studio in my house. He told me that he started selling drugs because he wanted to be like me. He liked my swag, saw the money I had, the attention I got and "no one messed with me," as he put it. He said, "I started selling drugs because I wanted to be like you." That's when I realized that my life was not about me, but about the legacy I would leave.

Most of us expect people to accept us as we are, saying, "Love me or hate me, but I am going to do me." We force people to accept and adopt our way of doing things if they want to have any kind of relationship with us. We force them to accept our principles, ideals, strongholds and issues with no intent of changing who we are so that we have better and more meaningful relationships. We accept the way we are as normal, without questioning whether the things we were taught shaped our current responses and choices.

CHAPTER 12

I Made a Choice!

Understanding our choices is perhaps the most important revelation to obtaining growth in many areas of our lives. Every time I responded unfavorably, I learned to question the response. I understood that to get the desired outcome, I must choose the best response. The result we want to see is based on our response to certain stimuli. Sometimes we don't always choose the best response and we can beat ourselves up about the choices we've made but understand this – how you choose is based on how you perceive your environment.

We are living in a war of the eyes, where perception rules our judgement. We are no longer guided by wisdom and understanding. We are controlled by our own self-righteous interpretations, which are not based on facts, but based on our own justified actions. Facts and truth no longer matter in this world. We live in a society where the best lie wins the argument and the truth is just a myth told by those whose lies have failed to stand against a theory.

Most people will believe a lie before they will accept the truth. In fact, most people prefer to be lied to than to be told the truth. People fear the pain that can sometimes be associated with truth, but why is that? Why has fear been coupled with truth, and peace with lies? If we take off the mask to see the face behind it and don't like what we see, we'll either have to change or put the mask back on. It's hard to comb through tangled or nappy hair but put a hat on it and no one can see the matted mess that you've covered up.

Society has convinced us to operate in the shadows of life, while the light has no workers. We have become a nation of followers who kill, diminish or decapitate those who desire to lead. Many are afraid to lead because they fear the castration of those who prefer to follow. Because of this, we have followers pretending to be leaders that receive guidance from leaders pretending to be followers.

Who and what are you ruled by? Does your perception revolve around the life you have lived, or is it guided by the life you *want or desire* to live? The answer to this question will determine who or what you will become or accept. Those who are guided by the life they've lived or the lives of others, will unfortunately only experience what they have seen; they will follow in the footsteps of their past perception.

Those who are fueled by the life they desire to have or live will undoubtedly experience new things, go to new places, have new trials and tribulations, break through new barriers and knock down new walls to see what's behind them. They will have new ideas and thoughts about life. They will be guided by the hand of their dreams and not by the feet of their circumstances.

Those who seek something they have never experienced will continue to encounter something they have never known. These same people will have to rely on a source that has experienced all things to get through the difficulties of their lives or they will need to find people who have done what they desire to do.

Choices are directly related to experiences. To make different choices you must experience something new. Choices are unknown if you don't understand what you have access to. No one goes to a chicken restaurant expecting to get crab legs. You are bound to choose only from what is on the menu, and if you want crab legs, you will have to go somewhere different.

As I started to question my responses, I started to understand that if I wanted to respond differently or if I wanted a different result, I had to do something that I had never done before. When the environment you're in no longer feeds your hunger, you must move to a place that can provide the nourishment you need to grow. What are you hungry for and where is it found?

Some animals migrate when they have consumed all the food in their natural habitat and there is nothing left for them to eat, grow and sustain life. Animals will travel thousands of miles in search of a reliable food source that meets their needs. How far are you willing to go to get what you need? Will you move forward to a new place or die in the habitat you're in after you've realized the current place can no longer feed your growth?

Changing your environment, mind and life is a choice. When a herd of elephants has no more food, a decision must be made by the leader to guide the herd to a better place where they can continue to produce, reproduce and thrive. If the elephants stayed in a place that could no longer feed them, they would die. When will you make the choice to change your current situation, so that you can produce something different?

The right to choose, in my opinion, is the most powerful thing in the world. Many people take their choices for granted, relinquishing them to the highest bidder and only getting pennies for that which really has no justifiably placed value. Who can really put a price or value on a choice?

Advertising agencies pay millions for your choices every day. They market products in places where you are most likely to see them, and bid for your choice, attempting to sway you one way or the other. People dress in the best garments to sway the choice of your eyes their way. People talk strategically, softly, loudly, to persuade your ears to listen. The softer it is the more likely you'll enjoy the touch of it on your skin. If it tastes the best, you'll want to eat it.

Options

Having the ability to choose gives you options. People will move mountains and even kill to have options. Having options is the difference between doing and not doing. Realizing your options helps you get the most out of your life. If all you have to eat in your environment are apples, you'll only know what apples taste like. What are your chances of trying an orange if suddenly introduced to one? Getting around the bitter obstacle of the orange's outer skin might deter some, but someone must step out and put away fear to try something different.

Someone has to be patient, diligent, and cautious enough, yet bold enough to try it. After a few tries, and when they have gotten to the sweet meat of the orange, seeing that it was good, that one who stepped out showed others that it was okay to do so. At that point, everyone who was introduced to an orange and accepted its taste, now realizes they have another option. The ones who accept the orange can now choose between an apple and orange. But those who chose not to accept the orange have chosen to limit their options to only an apple.

Accepting something new gives you the ability to make a choice. A choice can also be referred to as free will. A choice is the act of selecting or deciding when faced with two or more possibilities. Learning and understanding something new is the greatest thing you could ever do. Once I realized that I didn't have to be a homosexual male, before I ever became one, I was able to choose according to what was available to me; according to that which gave me the outcome I desired most.

If you don't understand your options, or see the possibilities, it's because you haven't desired and acquired something new and you can't make a viable choice. Where there are no options, we feel as if we must make an immediate choice. I decided to do something different. But what did that decision look like? How did I decide to change something that had been with me all those years? What does it mean to decide? To decide means to come to a resolution in the mind because of consideration. To consider means to think carefully on one thing, weighing options, pros and cons.

The principle of a choice is weighing out the options, as they pertain to a person, place or thing; narrowing down the possibilities by selecting the best options, then deciding amongst those to get the most desired outcome. This is what I call a 'decisive' decision. Being decisive means that the choices I make do not come with regrets. I fully understand all implications of the decision, whether it is the most desired outcome or the least. Either outcome should have been prepared for, because both should have been considered.

The choices I make shouldn't come with surprises. The choices that others make as they pertain to me, may come with surprises, but those choices I can't control; however, I can prepare for the most likely outcome of their choice and choose how to respond. Fighters prepare their defenses for the fight; they train and study the movements of their opponents. They study the possible actions of their opponents and prepare a response to their opponent's chosen action, based on the possibilities they already know about the opponent.

What you decide will ultimately determine your quality of life. If I chose to be happy, I'd be happy. If I chose to love, I'd love, even when hated or disliked.

Everything in life is a choice. People love to say, "I've made up my mind," and the truth is that there is no such thing as a made-up mind. If a person is presented with information that should change their way of thinking and it doesn't, that person is exhibiting a self-centered perspective. Most of us know it as being stubborn; however, being stubborn is another way of saying, "I want what I want," and guess what, you even must choose stubbornness.

Choosing New Information

We must accept new information and allow it to override the old. It's like getting an update to your cell phone. It's the same phone and program, but a different version of the program, which helps the phone operate efficiently or better in an ever-changing digital environment. Sometimes a program can update several times a week if there are things that changed suddenly. If we never update our phones, eventually they will start to operate poorly and inefficiently. If the phone continues to go without an update for an extended period, the phone could crash. Our brains are the same way. In my opinion, every time something changes around us, we should update our minds.

Just like the phone, our mind must be updated to operate efficiently in an ever-changing world. We see this displayed in a person who is just now getting a cell phone after only having a landline for years. They might have trouble with a flip phone, while the world is a decade ahead with touch screens. The user of the flip phone won't have access to the same features or options as the user of the touch screen, which means that their choices will be limited.

Not allowing new information to override old information immediately can cause stagnation. Accepting new information directly impacts your ability to make a sound and an accurate decision. A lot of people are living captive in their own minds because they hold on to old information, even though new information has been presented to them. I once thought I had to live a homosexual lifestyle because of being forced to do things with men as a child, but I realized that I am not a result of my circumstances, but a result of my choices.

Accepting New Information

Since my mind had been molested, changed and altered from its original intent or purpose, I had to find myself again. What was I created to do? Who was I created to be? I started with these basic questions. If I was to find myself, I had to start with what was guaranteed, not with what I felt like I was. What was a guarantee was that I was created and born as a man. I am naturally attracted to women, but I had been conditioned to accept men in a sexual manner. This was where I started. I accepted my truth and, while hard, it was my truth, nonetheless.

I was confused about what I was supposed to do, or who I was supposed to be, but I knew that I had a choice. My choice would be the deciding factor of who I wanted to become for the rest of my life. I wasn't raised in a religious background, so sin conviction didn't apply to my decisions.

To alleviate the confusion of my choices, I referred to my natural intent. As a man, I was created for reproduction purposes. It didn't matter how I felt, what was taught to me, or what they made me do, nature made me the seed depositor and a woman the receiver. If I was going to do what nature designed me to do, it would have to be with a woman. Now that I knew what to do, how do I do it? How do I turn what I know into an action?

To know something is to have information firmly in the mind committed to memory; to believe firmly in the truth or certainty of something; to be or become aware of something. When I became aware of new information, I had to figure out what to do with it. Do I immediately discard that information because it was unlike what I understood previously? Or do I verify that information and, if accurate, immediately start to implement the new information into my life?

I had this new information. I understood my original intent and I had to choose what I was going to do with it. Do I accept what I was conditioned to do, or do I do what I know I am supposed to do? Will I lead my thoughts or follow my thoughts?

Very few people are comfortable with change because of the fear associated with the unknown. Accepting new information will be hard, but submission and humility will help us to accept the fact that the truth as we know it may yet be a lie. Change does not exist in a place where new information is not accepted and implemented.

I understood that I had to submit to the change instead of fighting it. When I wanted to lose weight, I couldn't fight what I knew to do. I knew that I couldn't have those snack cakes. I couldn't eat everything I wanted to eat. I had to submit to doing something different. I had to accept the process and I had to choose to follow that process every day!

I couldn't make the choice a bit at a time and expect it to take me to the change I wanted to see. I couldn't expect one choice to get me through every day, hour or minute of possible temptation. I had to continue making the same choice every time I was faced with an obstacle or opposition. I accepted the fact that new information had been presented and allowed it to trump the old information. If applicable at that present time, I expelled the old information and adopted a new principle, based on the new information.

But I found it hard to accept new information at first because I got so much of it at one time and sometimes I didn't know what to do with it. I took in a lot of information daily and I had to allocate that information when it came in, so that when it was needed I knew exactly where to find it and how to use it.

How we process information will ultimately determine how we respond to a person, place or thing. Processing is a series of actions, directed towards a specific aim; a series of natural occurrences that produce change or development. I asked myself, "What series of actions do I use to compartmentalize my thoughts?"

I had to receive new information, question that information immediately, and even question my questions to see if they were valid; determine whether I could use the information right now or if I should store it for later. Sometimes I spent hours studying information that I couldn't use at the moment, instead of pouring that effort into gaining information about something I could immediately apply or use for personal growth and capital gain. There is nothing wrong with gaining random information, but I had to learn what information to focus on so that I could get the results I desired at that moment.

Information is something that never expires, but it always requires updating to retain its usefulness. I sat in a class for hours just to learn CPR. I gained the information and became licensed to use it, but I've never had to use the information I was licensed for, so right now it has no value. If I am on the beach and someone is pulled from the water in need of CPR, then at that very moment the value of the information I possess is immeasurable. Information has no value until it is used or has the potential to be used, not when it is obtained.

Information is like loose change. Some coins you put in your pocket because they have immediate or more value, like quarters, but other coins you put in a jar and save them until they have a higher value and are worth using, like pennies.

People are blackmailed because they fear certain information being used against them, not simply because it is possessed. Possession of information makes you a threat. Being a user of information makes you an enemy. The more important the information obtained, the greater the potential it has. Potential can't be utilized if there is no action taken after obtaining the information.

What would it profit me to have information and not use it? I could either use or pass it on to someone who may have an immediate use for it. How can I possess the knowledge to build a house and still be homeless?

I had the information I needed to get out of my current situation, but I either lacked the desire to act or I didn't know how to, which meant that I either needed motivation or instructions, and sometimes I needed them both. Information requires a plan to be used properly.

There were steps I had to follow in the CPR class to get to the desired outcome. Information without government or laws established can be dangerous. A person trying to administer CPR without training could cause death, whereas someone trained properly could save a life. A good deed done out of order because there is lack of training or preparation could kill. People have been sued pulling people from accidents because they caused more damage than someone trained to save lives would have done.

I learned to make choices only after I had considered the consequences. I thought about people who were in similar situations and asked what their outcome was. Was there anything written anywhere about what I am going through and, if so, where is it? Making a valid choice depends on the accuracy of the information received. No one should make a choice without being fully aware of all implications that come with the choice. Don't make wealthy-minded choices!

I grew up very underprivileged and I remember saying often that I wished I was like the rich. They go into the store and buy anything they want to. The wealthy don't check prices, they see it on the shelf, and because they know what should be available to them, they swipe their cards without question and look at what it was later while balancing their books, if at all.

Sometimes I could make decisions or choices like a wealthy person buying what they wanted. I made decisions without considering the consequences, like my bank of grace was endless. I decided without counting the cost of my decisions. I strolled through life's supermarket picking up choices and throwing decisions into my cart as if my bank account was consequence free. I had to understand that my choices are not like money. I can't just spend them at will and throw them out like I was making it rain in the club, because you don't get them back. Once a choice is made and an action is put behind it, you can't get it back. Choices can be forgiven, but they are often not forgotten.

There's nothing wrong with making a bad choice, but there is something wrong with constantly and consistently making bad choices. Well who's to say that my choice is wrong? Any choice that isn't conducive to the desired outcome you wish to see is by default a wrong choice. If I didn't get the result I wanted to see, it was a bad choice.

To desire means to want something very strongly. A result is something that follows as a consequence of an action, condition or event. That means that a desired result is a wanted consequence, condition or event. What do I want to happen? What do I want to come out of how I am about to respond? I started making choices based on what I wanted to happen more than I had ever done before.

You will always get the results of your decisions, unless there is intervention. I remember having confusing thoughts, thinking that I had to be with a guy, but didn't want to. I started to avoid men altogether. At football practice I didn't take showers with the rest of the guys because I didn't want to accidentally be attracted to them. I made a choice based on what I wanted to see, though I didn't understand the power of those choices at the time. Perhaps God was guiding my choices and I didn't know it.

Some might say I was running from who I was. I would say that is untrue because who I was had been altered when they molested my mind. I was conditioned to think a certain way, make certain choices and respond in a certain way; ways that were taught to me by the many circumstances and situations that rooted themselves as lessons in my life. That information was invalid information, false information that presented itself as though true. It wasn't what I was supposed to learn and, after obtaining new information, it was my responsibility to decide what I wanted to do with it.

I had many trials and tribulations that prompted certain choices, but once I understood the power of my choice, I made different ones. I didn't understand the choices I was making, I just followed the voice in my head that told me what was right and wrong. I listened to that voice because I didn't know what to do and it seemed to have all the answers; the first voice, not the second voice that usually questioned the first.

Having things taken or swindled from me affected the created version of who I was intended to be. After the day that David molested me, I was no longer the person that I was originally created to be. The second he stopped doing what he did, my life started changing. His choice affected my future options. Options had now been introduced to me that had not been there before, which meant that I could choose to be with a man or a woman. But what if the option of being with a man had never been presented to me? Would I have had a problem making a choice to be with a woman in the first place?

CHAPTER 13

I Have a Purpose?

Everyone has a basic purpose or intent that they were created or designed to be used for. Just like every animal has a specific design in nature, so too does every person. If you alter the DNA of their design, they will not function as intended in the same environment, and something that depended on them to function properly will not get what it needed.

Everyone must operate in their purpose or intent before their potential can be fully realized. Potential is defined as something that has latent possibility or likelihood of occurring, or of doing or becoming something. It is the capacity to develop, succeed or become something. Potential is invisible to an eye that does not have the capacity to hope or believe in something that is not seen. Potential is not guaranteed. Potential requires faith in something before it can come to fruition. A seed has the potential to become a tree, but before it can become what it needs to become, it must be placed in the right environment to reach its full capacity; it needs something from another source before it can become what it is meant to be.

Your potential is based in part on what you were taught, what was instilled in you, and your experiences throughout life. Our lives are mostly based on the ideals and teachings of other people. How many times do you stop to question those things called facts? Do you ever question what others have instilled in you, those things you were taught most of your life, the ideals that have formed who you have become today?

If you are like most people, you have never thought about what you think about and why you think about it. You may have never questioned why you made the decisions you've made. You might have just wandered through life helplessly making one decision after the other, never fully understanding how that decision would affect your life or your future potential.

When we are born, we are at the mercy of our environment. If you were blessed, you had a chance to grow up in a nurturing environment; a place where you were free to imagine and experiment; a place where you could try different things, see something new and experience culture at its finest.

As children, we are taught what others have already learned, those who guard us, teach us life's valuable lessons based on the lessons they've learned about life. Men teach their sons how to become men and their daughters about how men should treat them. Women teach their daughters how to become women and their sons about how women should treat them. How confident are you in the learning capacity of those who taught you some of your most valuable life lessons? What if your perception of life is based on the reality of their lives? People tend to tell someone else what can or can't be done because they could or couldn't do it, instead of advising them based on the probability of it altogether. Sometimes your perception of life is based on the reality of someone else's life.

Relying solely on someone else's direction is like deciding not to try new restaurants because of the reviews of others, not understanding that what tastes good to you might be different because of the different cultural adaptations that separate our decisions. You should always seek to guide your choices, not be led by them, and try to make choices based on more than one source of information to determine its truth.

I'll give you an example. Sarah had finally made it to high school, where she could fulfill her greatest dream of becoming a cheerleader. She had been waiting for this moment all her life; she had learned how to do a split, a cartwheel and a somersault. A week after school started, she came home and told her mom that she wanted to try out for the cheerleading squad and her mom started to laugh uncontrollably.

After Sarah's mom gained her composure, she told her daughter that she was too fat to be a cheerleader. Sarah's mom had tried out for the cheerleading squad in high school all four years, only to be denied every year because she couldn't lose 25lbs. She wanted to protect her daughter from the pain she had endured, so she spoke against her daughter trying out for the squad and said anything she could to deter her. Sarah never tried out for cheerleading and quickly gave up her dream because her mom constantly told her she was fat, that she would never make the team, and that she wasn't pretty enough. She said whatever she needed to say to prevent Sarah from trying out and being hurt, not realizing that she was doing more damage.

Sarah started to believe that she wasn't good enough for anything and gave up dreaming altogether. She started searching for ways to make herself feel good and that led to a host of bad decisions, including sex with multiple partners, and drugs. Sarah's potential was stolen from her by someone she trusted and loved the most. Now Sarah listens to her friends more than her parents. She developed love issues, truth issues, anger issues and insecurities, all because her mom thought she was doing the right thing.

Some of us don't know our potential because of invisible barriers that have been in place all our lives. These invisible barriers act in the way a traffic light, speed limit, stop or yield sign does as we travel this road called life. We have read the 'how to live' manual of the world and have conformed ourselves to its standards. It's like being born gave us a permit to live until we can understand what society expects from us to drive. We are tested and get a license to drive only when we abide by the rules and regulations of our peers.

Potential, Potential, Potential!

Before potential can be established, you must see it in your mind, you must envision it. You must be able to imagine what you want to see physically manifest itself. Few people go to the store and purchase a product they don't want, so why become someone you don't want to be? You can't walk a straight line without first seeing it or imagining it, but if you have never seen a straight line, you can't imagine one either.

After you have envisioned the 'potential you', before it can become something tangible, you must first design it. You must plan your potential. What will it take to become what I want to see? Most people will 'go for broke' without a list in the store. Have you ever heard anyone say, "Don't go to the store hungry?" People who don't make a list when grocery shopping tend to pick up things their stomachs desire and their eyes see. Some people can see something on other people that they like and adopt it as their own. No builder builds a house without first drawing a design and laying out the specs.

Don't think that you can haphazardly reach your potential without planning and following a set of steps to reach it. Determine whether what you see or like in someone else will fit your desired design. Decisions can be made in an instant; however, your potential can not. After potential has been envisioned and you've established a plan to achieve it, you must tune it.

The process of tuning a piano is the act of making minute adjustments to the tension of the strings to properly align the intervals between their tones. If you want to increase your potential, it must be constantly and consistently checked for functional ability. A car can run efficiently and yet still need to be tuned to run according to factory standards. Our potential is the same way; we can be operating in it but needing a tune-up.

Each time an adjustment or change is made to your potential, it must be tested. A manufacturer consistently put their products through rigorous tests in a controlled environment to see how they will perform in an uncontrolled environment. They prepare their products to handle the uses of the most destructive forces they can think of; tuning, tweaking and changing them when they find problems that could prevent them from being used as intended.

How much weight can your potential hold? What is its maximum strength? If you have the potential to become a millionaire, can you handle the pressure that comes with being a millionaire? Do you know how much you can take before you break, and have you prepared yourself in case you stop running as designed? Where do you go for parts? Who's your mechanic or engineer? What will be done if you find your potential broken?

You have envisioned your potential, designed it, tuned it and tested it. Now your potential is ready to be established. Establishing potential is a lot like putting the miles per hour radar on the dash of your car. The maximum amount of speed that your car's potential can sustain without failing is 160 mph. That means that if you desire to go the maximum speed of your car, you can. The car's potential was designed, tuned and tested for 160 mph. If you desire for your car to go any faster, you will have to modify it; change the body to make it a little more aerodynamic; modify the engine or replace it altogether; change the intake and exhaust. Sometimes you have to retune your potential during the establishing phase, retest it and determine its maximum output all over again. Have you ever wondered why you've repeated the same situations over and over again?

I realized that repetition also meant strengthening and building endurance. I used to think that failing, or feeling like I was failing, meant that I wasn't succeeding. But just like bodybuilders have to get their muscles to the point of failure before seeing gains, sometimes our potential is the same way. Failure can also be growth.

Due to the conditions of my environment, I may not be allowed to reach my full potential. Some environments may not be able to support the potential I have to offer. For example, my car can go 160 mph; however, the curve in the road can only handle 35 mph. Therefore, the speed I'm allowed to travel around the curve must be regulated and governed for the safety of those around me, as well as myself. Stop lights, traffic signals and signs are set in place to provide warning signs, promote caution and prevent accidents. Accidents, death and paralysis can occur when people break the regulations that govern misunderstood potential.

Your potential must be governed much like the car on the road. You can't just do what you want with your potential. You have a responsibility to those around you, to those who depend on your potential so that they can reach their full potential.

While governing is important for controlling your potential, one can only use the potential that has been obtained in an environment that will allow it to flourish. You can't fly a plane on the ground and you can't sail a boat on land. Have you at least reached your minimum potential? Maximum potential is reached in an environment where it is allowed. A car on the autobahn can reach its full potential because there is no speed limit.

Sometimes we need to get around people and places where we can just be ourselves; where no one will say, "That was a stupid thought," or "Why did you laugh?" or "Why did you say that?" Some place where we don't have to explain ourselves and we are free to just be. We need the right soil to grow in because everything can't grow in red clay. Some of us are trying to grow in stuff that's only good for making bricks or walls. Bricks aren't made to allow passage, they are made to hold things back. Bricks are designed to keep potential in and out. The walls you put up to protect yourself and keep people out, also trap you in, where your full potential can be hindered.

CHAPTER 14

I Was Saved

Even though I wanted to change, I still didn't have the power to do it on my own completely. I kept doing the things that I was doing before. I kept selling drugs. I kept making music and performing in strip clubs. I kept carrying weapons and planning licks. One day I decided that jacking dope boys was not getting me enough money. I didn't have enough manpower to hit anyone big because I didn't trust people, so I decided to do something that would get me the money fast.

I gathered a few young thugs that were under the radar and told them that we were going to rob a bank. I started making plans to rob a bank in a small town not too far away; a town that had fewer than five police patrolling at one time. It was a small bank that everyone used and fewer than five employees worked in at any one time.

I planned to cause a big fire in a big corn field in the town away from the bank; one that would tap-out the town's resources, leaving the bank vulnerable and the police unsuspecting; forcing all emergency crews to tend to the fire. I started compiling weapons and looking for a car that couldn't be traced back to me, but before I could go through with it, a knock came on the door.

I had been at my lowest point in life. I had lost everything that I held dear to me. I lost my car and couldn't get around the way that I needed to. I lost my job as a delivery driver, which was my cover-up gig. I lost my girl, so went my sense of hope. I was ready to sacrifice everything to get back on top. All the money that I made was spent daily and I didn't think about saving money for a rainy day; all I thought about was spending it as fast as it came in. So, when everything fell, it hurt me more than I could ever imagine.

I had lost my biggest buyers because I couldn't deliver their packages, and when a buyer is in need, you either had it or someone else did. All I thought about was getting back on top, so robbing a bank seemed to be my best option. I had grown up without having food daily, the water was off frequently, the lights were off even more frequently than the water, sometimes for weeks or maybe months. We never had a phone or cable TV. Most of my clothes had holes in them, my shoes talked more than a talented crackhead, and dirt was my only toy most of the time. We barely made it.

But now that I had the taste of money, I was willing to do what it took to keep it. Of course, I was nervous, but my need for money and getting my business back up again outweighed those nerves. I was sitting on a chair the week before I was to go through with my plans, and that's when I heard it, knock, knock, knock! I stood to the left of the door in case someone tried to shoot through it before kicking it in, then I asked, "Who is it?"

He said, "D!"

I said, "D who?" I couldn't make out the voice on the other side of the door.

He replied, "Deon, your cousin!"

I hadn't seen Deon in months. He used to run the streets, but after getting into some trouble out of town, he stopped coming around. We used to smoke, sell weed and hit the studio together, but he had stopped returning my calls after a while. I thought he had moved to ATL until he came by the house unannounced that day.

When I opened the door, I remember seeing a glow around him that I ignored at the time because I just thought he was happy to see me. We dapped each other up as he entered the house. I looked around outside after he walked in, then closed the door. We started making small talk and I asked him if he wanted to smoke. Deon told me no, he didn't want to smoke. I thought he was trying to get a job, so I asked, "You trying to get a job cuzzo, dats wuz up!"

He said, "Naw cuz, I just quit smoking."

Deon's answer surprised me, but I said, "Okay, dats wuz up, nothing wrong wit dat!"

As we talked, I kept noticing his smile, so I asked him, "Wuz going on cuzzo? Why you smiling so hard man? Wuz been up witchu my dude?"

He said, "Nothing man, just been chilling," but he kept smiling and looking at me funny. I was starting to get worried, because he looked so happy. I thought them boys might have gotten to him in jail or something and he was about to tell me he was gay now.

I asked him again, "What's going on with you cuz?"

He replied, "Nothing man."

I was getting frustrated a little and said, "Something bout you different cuz? Man, what's happenin witchu? Wuz going on man? Holla atcha boy!"

He sat up in the chair, looked me in my eyes, with tears starting to form, and said, "Well cuz, I found Jesus man."

I said, "Word!"

"Yeah man, and it's the best thing I could have ever done!" he replied.

I said, "Word, He make you feel like that huh?"

He replied, "Yeah man!"

For some reason a feeling came over me that I couldn't explain, something that I had never felt before. I started to get tears in my eyes. I started feeling sensitive and emotional. It was unfamiliar yet welcoming at the same time.

I looked at him and said, "If He makes you feel like that cuz, I want to find Him too!" Deon smiled at me, got up and gave me a hug, while shedding more tears. I didn't realize what finding Jesus really meant, but he invited me to church that Sunday and I went.

When I walked into the church I immediately started to cry. My aunt was the pastor of the church, the same aunt that made me eat that burger that I didn't want years ago. Everyone looked at me and I felt like I wanted to run, but they ushered me in and sang songs that seemed to touch the very core of my being. Then they asked me if I wanted to be baptized in the name of Jesus. I hesitated a little. My uncle told me what it meant to be baptized in the name of Jesus, and after a brief understanding, I said yes.

I was ushered into a room where I was to take off my clothes and put on a white robe. I was scared. I thought they were about to drown me. I wanted to change my mind; I wanted to scream, "STOP!" But the smiles, tears, clapping, and praising God kept me going. I climbed up the baptismal tub and stepped down in it, where my uncle was waiting for me. With tears in his eyes, my uncle told me to hold my breath and that it was going to be okay. He prayed for a few minutes and dipped me under the water.

I came out of the water and the weight of the world was gone; just like that, it was all gone! I wondered, how can I feel so free? How can things be so different? Why does everything look so different? What is this voice that I hear? What do I do now? Getting saved was not the easiest thing in the world to do, but it was the best thing I could have done. I thought getting saved meant that everything would be immediately better. I thought that everything would suddenly get easy and life would start over, but I was wrong.

It seemed like getting saved made life harder. I was used to doing everything I wanted to do with no real responsibilities to anyone other than myself. Now things were different. People looked at me differently, expected more from me and now I knew exactly what it meant when people talked about sin. The lessons came hard and fast. I learned that the voice of guidance that I had been hearing was not just my conscience, but God. This voice was something that Christians called, 'The Holy Spirit'.

This voice was the one leading me and causing me to ask questions. It was the voice that said, "You're running from something." I started to get the keys to life. The keys to the safe that I had been trying to unlock all my life were now being handed to me like a gift at Christmas. Answers to questions I hadn't known to ask were being presented to me. Lesson after lesson was being learned very quickly and they often came with many trials and tribulations. I was under the impression that when a person had gotten saved, they would enter a blissful state of living and be surrounded by peace and love. I quickly learned that as soon as you try to do right, wrong is right there with you.

About The Author

Quanjay Jaculb Jones

Born Quanjay Jaculb Jones on August 22, 1983. Quanjay grew up on the streets of Columbia, SC where he got used to life of crime, valuable lessons and hard experiences. Quanjay was raised by his mother, along with two sisters and two brothers. His early childhood years were filled with many trials and tribulations. By the time he was ten years old, he had already experienced many hardships in life and had gotten used to being under privileged. Quanjay was molested several times during his childhood years which left him scared, confused, angry and suicidal.

By the time he was eighteen years old he was well on his way to being a criminal. After many years of living the life he saw on the streets, Quanjay started writing poetry, producing music and rapping. Expressing himself through his music was where he found an escape from the world around him. After being incarcerated briefly behind the walls of a jail cell, Quanjay realized that wasn't the place for him, but it wasn't until he was introduced to Christ that he started to make changes to better himself and others around him.

Since being introduced to Christ, Quanjay has been in ministry for over eight years and has helped to change the minds and hearts of many through his teachings and powerful revelations. As a performing Christian Hip Hop Artist, Quanjay released his first album *Molested Minds* in 2015 and has since released several singles including *Blessed, Hakuna Matata,* and *Sheesh* under the artist name *Quanjay Lyon.* Quanjay is also a poet, producer and actor. He is an active participate of the program *Prison Fellowship,* where he commits himself and his heart to helping rehabilitate those who are incarcerated. For more info about Quanjay's music visit him on the web at www.QuanjayLyonMusic.com. If you would like to reach out to Quanjay with testimonies, you can reach him at theymolestedmymind@gmail.com.